2400 Jokes
to Brighten
Your Speeches

Also by Robert Orben

2100 LAUGHS FOR ALL OCCASIONS

2500 JOKES TO START 'EM LAUGHING

THE ENCYCLOPEDIA OF ONE-LINER COMEDY

THE AD-LIBBER'S HANDBOOK

THE JOKE-TELLER'S HANDBOOK

ORBEN'S CURRENT COMEDY
(a topical humor service for public speakers)

2400 Jokes
to Brighten
Your Speeches

Robert Orben

Doubleday & Company, Inc.
Garden City, New York
1984

Library of Congress Cataloging in Publication Data

Orben, Robert.
  2400 jokes to brighten your speeches.

  1. Public speaking. 2. American wit and humor. I. Title. II. Title: Twenty-
four hundred jokes to brighten your speeches.
PN4193.I5737 1984   818'.5402   83–25392
ISBN 0-385-17230-3

CONTENTS

Contents

viii   Contents

INTRODUCTION

"What are the odds?" It's a frequently asked question. It's perfectly normal to consider the risk-reward ratio in any new undertaking. What are the odds on a horse winning, a candidate being elected, a stock going up, a business succeeding? We weigh the evidence and then act accordingly.

So what are the odds on getting a laugh? If you're sold on the use of humor in communication, beware the tendency to be oversold. While humor can lighten and enlighten a situation—it may not be appropriate in every situation. The sensitive communicator should weigh the humor pros and cons of every speaking engagement. It's one way to keep your cream of wit from curdling.

First, let's consider the time of day. I've found that the chances of getting a laugh improve as the day grows older. Despite rumors to the contrary, most of us are imbued with the work ethic. Early in the morning there is an inbred motivation to get things moving, to accomplish. But humor calls for a certain amount of playfulness and relaxation. And so humor is a hard commodity to sell at breakfast meetings and midmorning events.

There are exceptions. If a joke is relevant and speaks to a common concern, it can work even at sunrise. I attended a breakfast at which President Ford was the speaker. The man who introduced him said that in his own military career, in World War II, he had spent four years getting up before the crack of dawn. And it wasn't his favorite hour. And so he vowed that when he got out of the army it would take the President of the United States to ever get him up at six o'clock in the morning again. A pause and then he added, "It's six o'clock. Ladies and gentlemen, the President of the United States!" Everybody in the room could relate to the thought and it worked. And so, if you have something that's right on the button for the time, the event, and the audience—you can get laughs from an early morning group. But it's much more of a challenge than later in the day.

Luncheon meetings and midafternoon sessions are worlds better for humor. The day is half over. Some amount of work has been completed. The trauma of commerce has been soothed by a 3-to-1 martini lunch. People are more receptive to fun and more willing to reward themselves with the luxury of a laugh.

But the best time of all is dinnertime and the evening hours. The battles of the day have been fought—and either won or lost—but, for the time being, they're over. People lean back and want to savor the things that make them feel good.

Laughter is one of them. Providing the Happy Hour is just happy and not uproarious, dinners and banquets are ideal vehicles for humor. We are conditioned to look on the evening as our time to enjoy. Dinner is served at eight. Serve the humor soon after.

The one storm warning to be aware of: the evening event that goes on too long. We've all sat through them. They're fun from seven to nine. Pleasant from nine to eleven. Torture from eleven to midnight. At every evening event there is a psychological optimum time to pack up the table tents and go home. If the program goes beyond this, even if you've prepared the funniest remarks and sagest speech ever—'tis best to throw in the towel and cut both your time and losses. Say something like "I've been sitting up here so long, the spotlight has faded my suit." Conclude with a sixty-second update of your speech and then lead the rush to the door. You'll be the hit of the evening.

Another important factor in the success of humor is the physical setting of the meeting or dinner. Get as close to the audience as possible. If the lectern is set far back from the first row of seats or tables, move it up. If you can't move it, work in front of it. Humor calls for involvement—attachment rather than detachment. What you are striving for is a one-to-one, eye-contact relationship with every member of the audience.

Some meeting planners either lose sight of the need for a physically close relationship between speaker and listener—or accept imposed conditions that make such a relationship difficult. A group of 200 in a meeting room that seats 500 is bad news. You just walk into that room and you sense failure. Two hundred may be the most attendees they've ever had, but in a room that holds 500 the audience looks like a quota that hasn't been met.

Further, laughter is a social exercise. If you hear the person next to you laughing out loud, you are more apt to do the same. And so it's important that your room be just big enough to encompass your group—and the number of chairs available just enough to seat them. Better to scrounge for more chairs from another location if they are needed than to have your audience scattered about the room like chips on a chocolate cookie. Your listeners should be able to relate to you and also to each other. The natural impulse upon hearing an apt, relevant joke is to nudge someone in agreement. You've got to have someone close enough to nudge.

Laughter feeds on laughter. That's why most TV shows have laugh tracks. The laugh track of the capable speaker is an audience responding to a properly written and told joke. If the audience is seated in a room just large enough to hold it comfortably, the laughter bounces off the walls and reverberates throughout the room. It becomes contagious. It *sounds* as if everybody is having such a good time, if you're not laughing maybe *you're* wrong.

In essence, effective humor should be like a party with everyone joining in the fun. But sometimes a party suffers if there are too many or too few people. The same holds true when you're looking for laughs. If an audience is too small, each member is more aware of the others and, as a result, feels less comfortable. Emotional protection is provided by the crowd and that is lost in a group of five or ten. Since laughter calls for a certain amount of "letting go," the smaller the group the harder the going.

Conversely, when your audience numbers in the thousands, it just isn't possible to maintain eye contact and a sense of togetherness. A curious mix of reactions greets comedy performed in the huge show rooms of Las Vegas or in the mammoth civic auditoriums now being built. Most of the laughter comes from the semicircle of audience within easy eye contact of the performer. The rest may be enjoying the performance, but they aren't obligated to show it. And if you study the audience in the far reaches of the second balcony, even comedy superstars are being met with silence.

Speakers can learn a lesson from this: lighten or eliminate the humor load whenever audiences are too large for personal interaction. The jokes that *do* work before a large mass of listeners tend to be jokes that speak to a fervently held common interest or concern. If it's a political rally, needling the opposition never fails. If it's a graduation exercise, belittling the traditional sports rival is surefire. But more general humor tends to be lost in and by the crowd.

Outdoor events are another problem for the joke-teller—and the serious speaker as well. The attention and the interest span of outdoor audiences are limited. They're with you for five to ten minutes and then their interest is off and running with the first passing airplane or child crying. Jokes suffer because of the absence of a roof and four walls to contain the sound. As a result, even a big laugh sounds weak as it wafts off in all directions. A good general rule is to follow the KISSSSS formula for outdoor events: Keep it Short, Simple, Sincere, and Semi-serious.

Finally, let's talk about the audience—the focus of any speaker's attention. As any performer will tell you, there is no constancy in audiences. They may look the same but the chemistry of audiences —their interest and receptivity—varies greatly. The same jokes, the same speech, the same performance can get a standing ovation one night and yawns the next. For six years I was a writer on the Red Skelton TV show in Hollywood. We had a sign on our office wall that cut short all complaints about any problems we encountered. It said: IF IT WAS EASY, YOU WOULDN'T BE MAKING ALL THIS MONEY.

Assessing an audience is neither easy nor an exact science—but certain generalities, based on experience, can be established. If I had to rate the receptivity of audiences, all-female audiences would head the list; male-female audiences would place second; all-male audiences third. Obviously, each group can be and is responsive to humor—but each requires a slightly different approach.

Without going into psychological theories, I have found that audiences of women are apt to be more relaxed and have a greater willingness to be entertained. Providing the humor isn't sexist, they respond to a wide variety of subject matter.

The mixed-gender audience offers a little more resistance. The couples respond to the material and to the speaker, but they are also aware of their partner's reaction to the performance and their partner's reaction to their own response. General humor works, but a little more attention to material that speaks to the audience's shared interests is wise.

The all-male audience may present the biggest challenge in doing humor. Humor is power. Humor is control. When we laugh, we temporarily give ourselves over to the person who makes us laugh. A lifetime of macho conditioning makes a male reluctant to do this. And so the best humor for all-male audiences are jokes that bond the speaker to the audience and take a supportive and affirming humorous stance on subjects of common and intense interest: sports, politics, shared problems.

Just as the capacity to enjoy humor improves as the day grows older, it also improves as the audience grows older. Young audiences—those in their teens and early twenties—have a limited range of interests and experience. Their laughter is more a vote than a sign of enjoyment. If a joke supports the traditional rebellions of youth, it'll work. Antiauthority; antiestablishment; prodrug; prosex; iconoclastic put-downs are what turn on many young audiences.

As people grow older and more secure—or at least become less intimidated by the newness of life—they tend to be more accepting of their own foibles and foolishness. They see more of the humor that is in each and every one of our lives. And so perhaps the best audiences of all are the older ones. Those who have made an accommodation with life and have mulched any chips that might have been on their shoulders. Today, tonight, this meeting, this show, is for enjoyment. Let's get on with it!

The mood of the audience is the ultimate key to your success. One of the most difficult nights I ever experienced in a theater happened in 1962. I was a writer on the Jack Paar prime-time TV show and Jack was taping a show on the night the Cuban missile crisis was coming to a head. Russian ships were approaching the U.S. naval blockade points and the expected confrontation could well have led to World War III. There wasn't a member of Jack's audience who wasn't fearful that this night might end with a nuclear holocaust.

As it happened, Russia blinked first—and, frankly, so did Comedy. Jack Paar's talent, charisma, and sensitivity kept the show and the evening afloat, but it had to be one of the most subdued audiences in history. Because the primary purpose of Jack's show was comedy, there was no way to sidestep the humor. But there are times when a speaker is faced with this same type of preoccupied, inwardly directed audience. If so, forget humor. The odds are against it.

So, before you use humor, consider the odds—and if you can, try to stack them in your favor. In Las Vegas it's the way to beat the house. In speaking, it's the way to bring down the house.

And now please turn to and enjoy more than 2400 jokes that are odds-on to brighten your speeches, your conversation, and your reading.

Bob Orben

2400 Jokes
to Brighten
Your Speeches

AIRLINE FARES

God must have loved airline fares. He made so many of them.

Have you been out to the airport lately? They now have an express line for flights with six prices or less.

Airlines now have nine basic fares: FIRST CLASS, ECONOMY, TOURIST, COACH, NIGHT COACH, SAVER, SUPER SAVER, STANDBY, and MAKE-US-AN-OFFER.

Where else but in America could you spend $229 and be called a "super saver"?

And I'll never understand first-class fares. If you fly to Europe, you pay another $800 and what do you get? Fourteen inches more of leg room. I mean, who can stretch that good?

I don't want to complain about the difference between coach and first-class fares, but I once flew first class and when the stewardess came over I whispered something in her ear. She just smiled and said, "You got that when you bought your ticket."

The airlines think of everything. They've now made it possible for those of you who have always wanted to go to Europe in the worst possible way to do so. It's called Standby.

I finally figured out why the airlines call it "Standby." That's what you do at the gate as the plane takes off.

As you know, November 23rd is a very special day for America. It's when the last of the Standby passengers come home from Europe.

AIRLINES

America is where we have an airline that's United and a government that isn't.

It's all in the way you look at it. All of my life I've flown in company planes. The companies they belonged to were American, T.W.A., and Delta.

I love to fly because stewardesses are really fun people. A stewardess is someone with a smile on her face, a sparkle in her eyes, and 300 little bottles of liquor in her pantry.

If you really want to irritate a stewardess, when she asks you to put your seat in an upright position, stand on your head.

Do you ever get the feeling that airline baggage handling was invented by Orville and Wilbur Wrong?

AIRLINE SEATING

Scientists say you can't put more into a container than the container will hold. Now if we could only convince the people who design airline seats.

The airlines are crowding so many people into a plane, the newest economy fare calls for alternate-side-of-the-aisle breathing.

I love those planes that have the five seats in the middle, an aisle on either side, and then more seats. It's like flying to Europe in your dentist's waiting room.

In 1903, Wilbur and Orville Wright invented a plane that only held one person. Now we have planes with *seats* that don't even hold one person.

The airlines are making seats that are so narrow, turning the other cheek isn't a virtue, it's a necessity.

I love to travel by plane. If you hear a pop, it's either a cork coming out of a bottle in first class or a passenger coming out of a seat in tourist class.

I don't mind the airlines crowding so many people into such narrow seats, but at least they could make it boy, girl, boy, girl. I have enough vices now I can't satisfy.

If airlines put people any closer together, they're going to have to do one of two things: either put saltpeter in the coffee or mirrors on the ceiling.

You don't know what it's like to spend seven hours flying to Europe sitting in the middle seat—and on either side of you are people with samurai elbows!

The captain says, "If you look to your right, you'll be able to see Paris and the Eiffel Tower." I look to my right and all I can see is an earring and wax!

The worst seat you can have on a plane is an aisle seat, because all the food and drinks and snacks have to go over you to get to the other passengers. And, as we all know, the only time airlines ever serve food is during a typhoon alert. . . . One time the person sitting in the window seat asked me what we were having for dinner. I said, "Wait a minute. I'll look in my lap!"

I'm firmly convinced that if God had meant us to have airline seating He never would have given us knees.

Airplanes are now divided into two sections: SMOKING and NO SMOKING. In Italy the planes are also divided into two sections: GARLIC and NO GARLIC.

AIRPLANES

I understand the manufacturers of aircraft stand behind every plane they sell. I'd be more impressed if they stood under them.

Metal fatigue is when you talk about an important part wearing out. I get enough of that from my wife.

The big concern in airline circles is how the engines are mounted. Personally, I feel that what mechanics do in the privacy of their own hangars is their business.

Remember your first flight and how you spent the entire time looking out the window—watching, listening, and worrying about the engine? Remember your last flight and how you spent the entire time looking out the window—watching, listening, and worrying about the engine?

It used to be that I'd get on a plane and I'd be a white-knuckle flier. Now I'm close to albino.

And I'm not the only one. It's the first time I ever heard a stewardess offer coffee, tea, or Greyhound.

You can always tell the atheists in a plane. They wear little F.A.A. medals around their necks.

ANTIQUES

An antique shop always gives me the feeling I'm walking around in my wife's handbag.

My brother-in-law is never going to make it in the antique business. Yesterday he threw away a blotter that had been used at the signing of the Declaration of Independence—because John Hancock's signature was written backward.

He just paid $500 for what has to be one of the most valuable historical documents of all time. Remember how Moses took down the Ten Commandments on two tablets of stone? He bought the carbon copy!

I don't think that painting of Adam and Eve at the local art museum is too authentic. For instance, Adam is wearing a fig leaf with a zipper.

APARTMENTS

You know why they call them "luxury apartment houses"? After you pay the rent, you can't afford any!

They do everything to make these new luxury apartment buildings the ultimate in refinement, good taste, and dignified living. For instance, the cornerstone says M-C-M-L-X-X-X-IV. That's Latin for CURB YOUR DOG!

Have you looked at apartments lately? All the new buildings are forty stories high. Now you can get an apartment and a nosebleed at the same time! . . . I looked at one yesterday. It's only two miles from shopping—straight down!

This building is so tall, I was riding up in the elevator and as we were going past the hundred and third floor I said, "Good Lord!" And a voice answered, "Yes?"

They're putting up one building that's so high, the elevators are by Boeing!

ARMY

These will be great years for the Pentagon. To the average citizen, a stockpile of tanks, guns, and missiles is frightening. To the Pentagon, it's Toys-R-Us.

I saw a picture of that new tank that can go 45 miles an hour, has 6-inch armor-plate, a 105-mm cannon—and, thanks to our defense budget, the army will have 10,000 of them by 1985. Not the tank, the picture.

This tank will cost $1.1 million each—radio and heater extra.

I know that sounds like a lot of money but it isn't easy buying a tank. You ever kick a tread?

There's got to be a way of reducing this price—cutting out some of the frills. I mean, does a 60-ton tank really need curb feelers?

Women should register for the draft because they're much healthier than men. When they go down for their physical, you never hear them coughing.

Obviously, women in the armed services have brought about some changes. For instance, creamed chipped beef on toast is now called by a rather strange name—creamed chipped beef on toast.

I think it's a mistake not to allow women to go into combat. Why let all those years of marriage go to waste?

I was never much of a soldier. My idea of a cadence count was: "Help! Two. Three. Four. Help! Two. Three. Four."

I could never get used to the army wardrobe. I mean, who wears olive-drab undershirts and olive-drab shorts? I looked like a sex symbol for frogs.

Now everything's changed. Now it's the "new army." I didn't realize how new until I went into the mess hall. The one with the strolling violinist.

ATLANTIC CITY

A lot of people are planning to spend their vacations in Atlantic City, which is very appropriate. A vacation is where you get away from it all—and Atlantic City is where they get it all away from you.

I can remember when you went to Atlantic City to get tanned. Now you go to get faded.

Atlantic City has always had gambling. Ask anyone with dentures who has ever eaten salt water taffy.

Gambling has really done wonders for the Atlantic City economy. It's the first time I ever saw slot machines that take welfare checks.

Then there's the New Jersey resident who started saving a year ago. She skipped lunches, ate peanut butter sandwiches for supper, brought deposit bottles back, took on a paper route, gave up movies and cigarettes, cut down on her kid's allowance, made do with last year's clothes—and on the first day of legalized gambling went to Atlantic City with $900. Pushed her way up to the roulette table, put the entire $900 on red—and lost. And as she left was heard to say, "Well—easy come, easy go!"

I understand a Salvation Army band was asked to move away from the entrance to a casino in Atlantic City. It was either that or stop playing "Bringing in the Sheep."

AUTO INDUSTRY

I don't think there will be an auto strike because this year Detroit has a secret weapon to keep workers from going home—the new TV season.

Detroit isn't too optimistic about the future. I happen to know that optional equipment on the 1985 models will be a bus ticket.

Things are a little rough now, but I think American cars are going to be around for a long, long time. I'd bet my Packard on it.

One company is really making fantastic deals on their new models. I saw a dealer pull up to a toll booth on the New Jersey Turnpike. The collector said, "Two seventy-five"—and the dealer said, "Sold!"

I always enjoy talking to people in the automobile industry because they really know how to concentrate on business. Last month I was at a dinner for auto dealers, and the minister who was supposed to deliver the invocation didn't show up. When they got to that part in the program the toastmaster turned to one of the auto dealers and asked him to say a prayer. The dealer said he didn't know any prayers. The toastmaster said, "Then do something religious." So he raffled off a Cadillac!

AUTO MECHANICS

Remember the good old days—when a supercharger was part of the car? Now it's the guy who makes out the bill!

Auto repair estimates always come in two stages: $30 when you bring the car in and $462 when they call you on the phone an hour later. . . . Now I know why Alexander Graham Bell's first words on the phone were: "Mr. Watson, come here; I want you." What he wanted was a loan.

A do-good organization is now training hookers to become auto mechanics because it's such a logical transition. Same position, same prices.

Have you noticed how auto mechanics always seem to have certificates and diplomas on their walls? And they really explain a lot. For instance, my mechanic majored in Estimates with a minor in Head Shaking and Uh-oh.

Auto mechanics really have it made. Name me one other business that can nick you for $500 and not even be afraid to leave fingerprints.

The thing that has always impressed me about auto mechanics is their sense of dedication. It's really amazing, when you bring your car in for service, that in the course of changing five quarts of oil they can also determine that the bearings in the rear trapezoid linking the transmission assembly with the differential calculus is worn. . . . It's almost a mystical experience, like the laying on of hands. Only what they're laying them on is your wallet.

I've found that auto mechanics who are hard of hearing are the most honest. You ask them, "Does my car really need all this work or what?" And they say, "What?"

My auto mechanic gets very upset watching that Mr. Goodwrench commercial. He can never understand why Mr. Goodwrench is always wiping his hands on a rag when there are perfectly good seat covers right in front of him.

Have you noticed how some auto mechanics love to wipe their hands on your seat covers? You drive your car out of the garage and it isn't long before you discover the Black Bottom is more than a dance.

AUTUMN

This is really going to be a glorious fall. We can already see three things turning yellow—the trees, the leaves, and investors.

September is the month we see all the back-to-school sales. In stationery stores for the kids—in liquor stores for the teachers.

The brilliant colors of autumn are the first signs of decay that will soon turn into rot—as anyone who has watched the new TV season will tell you.

October is when I get the awful feeling our Sales Department couldn't sell a rake in Vermont.

October is the moment of truth, when you go to get your winter clothes out of storage. Let's face it, to you it's a clothes closet. To moths, it's McDonald's.

BABIES

Doctors are once again coming around to the belief that mother's milk is best for babies. They cite four reasons: it's nutritious, inexpensive, emotionally satisfying, and there are no crumbs.

I still can't figure out why baby food should have such adult prices.

The woman next door just had a multiple birth. She said it was her first—and her last.

A couple who has six babies in a row is suffering from diaper rush.

A mundane thing has happened,
But now the fun begins;
Our neighbor who works for Xerox
Just became the father of twins.

We were so poor, we couldn't afford baby powder, so they sprinkled me with flour. You should have seen me on a hot day. I was the only kid in town who broke out in bagels!

I was a good baby. I was such a good baby they called me Martini. I was extra dry!

A heating oil supplier was talking to an obstetrician about the record cold winter. He said, "January was my busiest month ever. People just stayed home and tried to keep warm." The obstetrician nodded, "Mine will be October. Same reason."

BABIES (TEST-TUBE)

I just got back from an extremely sophisticated wedding. There were three items on top of the wedding cake—a bride, a groom, and a test tube.

I dunno. Somehow I never expected conception to be a spectator sport.

I'm a traditionalist. I feel that anyone who makes babies in a test tube has got it glass backward.

Today we have come together to discuss one of the most difficult, one of the most complex, and one of the most controversial questions of our time: do test tubes need foreplay?

It's really incredible what science is doing. I just saw a test tube with stretch marks.

Of course you can have babies from a test tube—but will they respect you in the morning?

I don't want to brag, but I knew something was going on when I saw that test tube with a mirror on the ceiling.

I don't know what's happening to this world. Yesterday I heard a test tube singing: "Yes, Sir, That's My Baby."

I wonder if test tubes ever have headaches?

BAIL-OUTS

As a taxpayer, I'd like to ask one question: why is it that, every time someone gets bailed out, we have to pay for the pail?

A bail-out is when your tin cup runneth over.

I knew this would happen and it's all because of automatic transmissions. We've forgotten how to shift for ourselves.

BALDNESS

IF YOU'RE BALD: I asked the Program Chairman what he wanted me to talk about and he said, "Oh, just let your hair down." So right away I knew I was in trouble.

Life is a series of unfulfilled dreams. For instance, I always wanted to wear my hair long. At least, a lot longer than I did.

It isn't easy being bald. Who else do you know has to wear prescription dandruff?

I'm not criticizing baldness because—and not many people know this—there happens to be a religious reason for baldness: God in His infinite wisdom has created millions and millions and millions of heads—and those He's ashamed of He covers with hair.

BANKS

I'm getting a little worried about our neighborhood bank. Yesterday one of my checks came back marked INSUFFICIENT FUNDS. I mean, what kind of a bank is it that doesn't have twenty-five bucks?

Banking, like government, is basically a system of checks and balances. If you want to write a check you have to have a balance.

Lending money is always a risky business. You don't know how it feels to see someone sign a promissory note for two million dollars and then wipe his fingerprints off the pen.

I used to deal with one bank that was so shaky, even its cash bounced!

They claimed they had assets of roughly $200 million. When you smoothed it out it was $1.75 and three toasters.

You couldn't help but be a little suspicious when they gave you a choice of three scenic checkbooks: the Mississippi River, the Rocky Mountains, and Leavenworth.

Maybe this is being negative, but I can't help but think that if God had meant us to have banks Moses would have come down from Mount Sinai with the Ten Toasters.

I went in to get a loan from a trust company and it was a very educational experience. I learned that the trust was mostly on one side.

The one thing that has always bothered me about banks is the total lack of a reciprocity of trust. I mean—you give them $10,000 and all you get in return is a certificate—and they put chains on twenty-five-cent pens that don't work!

Have you ever tried to write with a bank pen? I don't really think they're pens. They're more like blue ketchup bottles. . . . You shake them three times and then SPLAT!

I had dinner at my banker's house on November 22nd and it was very unusual. The first time I ever celebrated Thankslending.

Every problem has a solution. Chefs cover their mistakes with sauces; surgeons cover their mistakes with earth; and international bankers cover their mistakes with loans.

You can always tell the banks charging 13% interest by one thing: the TV camera that photographs robberies is on the loan officer.

BANQUETS

To avoid any distractions during the speeches that follow the banquet, we have taken the liberty of serving you, for dessert, an ice cream with a very unusual flavor—Rolaid.

Fund-raising banquets are where you get service with a smile. The waiters can't get over what you're paying for that food.

I'm always shook up by those fancy dinners where the waiters wear gloves. You can't help but wonder, "What's in the food they're afraid to touch?"

Banquet service is when you have more elbows in your mouth than food.

A typical banquet is where the red is always served at room temperature. Sometimes it's the wine. Sometimes it's the strawberry ice cream.

Wasn't that a fantastic dinner? I have only one suggestion: the next time, make the after-dinner mints Tums.

There's a pattern to banquets. For instance, when you sit down, if the appetizer, salad, and dessert are already on the table, it means one of two things: either the program is long or the budget is short.

What most banquets need is an express podium—for speakers with six thoughts or less.

I just figured out why chicken is so often served at banquets. Like the speeches, chickens rarely get off the ground.

It's always a thrill speaking at a golf banquet. Where else can you see people holding the microphone with an interlocking grip?

BASEBALL

I may skip baseball this year. I don't think I could take one more strike.

Yesterday I went to the ball park and paid seventy-five cents for a bag that contained twelve peanuts. There's even a song about it: "Take Me out at the Ball Game."

My wife had a very upsetting thing happen yesterday. She was watching Julia Child on television; somehow it got mixed up with the (CELLAR BASEBALL TEAM) game—and she wound up with three cake batters that struck out.

I used to root for a team that was always making excuses. Whenever someone sang " 'Oh, say, can you see?' "—the outfielders claimed they were blinded by the sun.

It's always discouraging to see the best hitter on your team raise a cup of water to his lips—and miss.

Life is unfair. Do you realize that in the last six months the Mafia had more hits than the (LOSING BASEBALL TEAM)?

Seattle is a great place to play baseball. In most towns, if a pitcher doesn't do well, he goes to the showers. In Seattle, the showers come to him.

BEACH

Sunday I went to the beach and one girl was wearing a pale blue mini-bikini. She said, "It brings out my eyes." I said, "It brings out mine too!"

I can never understand why fellas take girls to the beach because the first thing girls do when they get to the beach is smear oil all over themselves. It's like dating Saudi Arabia.

The whole point of suntan lotion is, it keeps people from getting burned. Forget the beach. Use it on Wall Street!

I had a terrible experience at the beach today. I found a seashell, held it up to my ear, and it said, "Sell!"

Timing is everything in business. I don't care how well financed it would be. I don't care how well advertised it would be. I don't care how well managed it would be. Now is not the right time to open a nude beach in Anchorage, Alaska.

BEES

I was reading a book about killer bees who attack everything in sight. You can't blame them for being mad. Somebody called their leader a queen.

The bees travel thousands and thousands of miles and, when they arrive, they want to kill. I've had flights like that myself.

It's really an incredible thing. Have you ever heard ten billion bees buzzing in unison? Sounds like the Mormon Tabernacle Choir in heat!

But we should keep our perspective on bees. Let's face it, to us a bee is an insect. To a flower, it's Robert Redford.

I'm in advertising. I really don't know much about bees. Their sons, yes.

BEVERLY HILLS

I just got back from doing a benefit for the boat people of Beverly Hills. That's anyone who owns a rowing machine.

There's no question that the rich are different. In Beverly Hills, a terrorist organization is the I.R.S.

I once went to a stock car race in Beverly Hills and it was really exciting. In the very last lap a Rolls beat out a Bentley.

In Beverly Hills, they have their own idea of what a car pool is. It's a Winnebago with a diving board.

People in Hollywood get married so many times, it's incredible. I once went to a P.T.A. meeting in Beverly Hills that had 400 parents for 16 kids!

I love Beverly Hills. Where else can you see kids making mud pies in a Cuisinart?

Kids in Beverly Hills put on their own Christmas pageant and the first scene, in particular, was fascinating. It showed Mary and Joseph going to Bethlehem to pay their taxes. One little girl was Mary, one little boy was Joseph, a fat kid was their donkey, and a kid with glasses was their C.P.A.

Everything in Beverly Hills is different. Name me one other town where you can send your kids to Little League option trading.

Here's a late-breaking item: flooding continues in Mississippi, Texas, and Beverly Hills. A Perrier truck sprang a leak.

They really have style in Beverly Hills. Where else can you see Kool-Aid being made with Perrier?

Have you ever gone into a Beverly Hills funeral home? It's fascinating. Perhaps the only place in the world where you can buy a casket with a swimming pool.

BILLS

They now have an institution for people who get invoices from the electric company, the heating oil company, and the property tax office, all on the same day. It's called The Home for the Terminally Billed.

The most important thing you learn around the first of the month is—any envelope that comes with a window isn't worth looking into.

We've had one of those years where every day I light my cigars with hundred-dollar bills. Some are sixty days overdue. Some are ninety days overdue.

BLACKOUTS

I had a funny experience in (BLACKED-OUT CITY). At exactly (TIME) on (DATE), I was trying on a pair of sunglasses.

What makes everybody so sure that at (TIME) on (DATE) God didn't look down at (BLACKED-OUT CITY) and say, "I'm mad as hell and I'm not going to take it anymore!"

There's a new theory as to what might have caused the blackout. Maybe somebody was using Grecian Formula and forgot to say when.

Is it true that in (BLACKED-OUT CITY) A.C. doesn't mean Alternating Current? It means Always Chancy.

They're beginning a massive investigation into the monumental forces that caused the blackout. First: who put the penny in the fuse box?

"It is better to light one small candle than to curse the darkness."
"Who said that?"
"Mayor (OF BLACKED-OUT CITY)."

BLIZZARDS

What this country really needs is a timed-release blizzard.

The biggest problem with a blizzard is when you run out of basic food items and have to improvise. You ever tasted Twinkies au gratin?

Being stranded in a blizzard is a unique experience. It's like living in the vanilla machine at Dairy Queen. And California is having mudslides. That's like living in the chocolate machine at Dairy Queen.

BOOKS

Have you read ——————? It's over 1000 pages. It's a coffee table book—if you have a very strong coffee table.

You've heard of books that you can't put down? This one you can hardly lift up!

It's the kind of book you wouldn't want to leave around where the kids could get at it. Who needs an eight-year-old with eyestrain and a hernia?

There are two things in this book that really make you stand up and cheer. One is THE and the other is END.

BOSSES

Laugh and the world laughs with you. Cry and you've learned the boss was going to tell that same joke.

The boss is getting a little cynical. His latest theory is that deficits are catching. You get it from your salesman.

Our boss is all thumbs—and there's an employee under each of them.

The boss is a firm believer in fireside chats. If you don't take his side during a chat, you're fired.

The most difficult task a boss ever has is to fire a gofer. How do you tell someone they flunked Flunky?

The boss has just about completed a warm, caring, heartfelt Christmas message to his staff. All he has left to do is look up the spelling of "flunkies."

> I've come to this conclusion,
> It's one I've long supposed:
> The boss's door is open—
> It's his mind that's always closed.

You may have seen my boss. He's the one with the walk-in mouth.

Our boss is really progressive. You know how some companies have the four-day workweek? He believes in the four-week workday!

The boss paid my creativity a rare compliment today. He said I never make the same mistake twice—I'm always searching out new ones.

I'll never forget the time the boss said I had a minuscule command of the English language, was incredibly slow on the uptake, and was completely oblivious of what was going on around me. Fortunately I had an answer for him. I said, "Huh?"

For those of you who have never met the boss, he's the one with the walk-in wallet.

Due to the vicissitudes of the fiscal markets, the boss is in a holding mode that obviates the disbursement of superfluous seasonal remuneration. Or, to use the generic term—cheap.

When it comes to the holidays, our boss is a traditionalist. He always has one thing that's marked DO NOT OPEN UNTIL CHRISTMAS. It's his wallet.

It's always easy to spot the boss at an office party. He's the one who gets the cringing ovation.

BUDGETS

Most government budgets are like the bacon you buy in supermarkets. There's a little meat on top and a lot of fat underneath.

Where else but in Washington could one federal agency ask for $5 billion—another ask for $10 billion—and have the Office of Management and Budget complain it's being nickeled and dimed to death?

Economists have been urging the President to take emergency action to balance the budget—and he is. Beginning April 1st, the United States will go condo.

The President's new budget calls for spending $————— billon. $————— billion! No use talking—somebody's got to tell him about K-Mart.

DON'T BALANCE THE BUDGET. TILT THE COUNTRY!

I once heard the liberal philosophy of government defined this way: every time the government moves to the left, the decimal point in the federal budget moves to the right.

What this country really needs is a peanut butter federal budget— one that sticks to the roof of the Treasury.

The President has proposed a $————— billion federal budget. I can't even imagine $————— billion. I mean, I have teenagers who couldn't spend that much.

Can you imagine how a taxpayer feels when he reads about a $————— billion budget—and he's making dinner with Leftover Helper?

A senator got a phone call from one of his constituents who said he had been reading about the new federal budget. He said, "Senator, I'm just curious how long you figure it will take the government to spend $————— billion?" The senator said, "Just a minute," and turned to look it up. The caller said, "That's what I thought," and hung up.

The defense budget for 19——— could be as high as $————— billion. I think we've finally managed to put peace on a wartime basis.

BUSINESS

I'm getting a little worried about our accounts receivable. Last week we had to put antifreeze in our cash flow.

No two snowflakes are alike. We have a production line with that same problem.

A consultant is someone you pay a hundred dollars an hour to give you the same advice you ignore from your assistant.

Why is it that, when an opportunity is lost, it's usually your competitor who finds it?

I always make it a point to try to love our competition—because you always hurt the one you love.

A company can always make it through thick and thin providing the thick isn't their executives and the thin isn't their capital.

When it comes to playing hard to get, you just can't beat profits.

Everything is relative. To the business world, it's an industry-wide price hike. To the consumer, it's no-fault greed.

It's just amazing how quickly the Administration has restored business confidence. You go into any steel company and they're confident they're getting the business.

If your business is going to hell, big government is often the travel agent.

It's rather hard to describe our industry. Picture a nervous breakdown with paychecks.

The employees of our company have just been given some good news and some bad news. The good news is, the Chairman of the Board's door is always open. The bad news is, we can't afford a lock.

All right, who's the wise guy who referred to our annual report as the digital crock?

I won't say how our company is doing but it's the first time I ever heard taps played during an annual report.

I don't mind telling you, I'm worried sick. I just heard our Treasurer singing: "You're my kind of town, (BANKRUPT CITY) is."

The big problem in doing business today is—everybody wants Microwave deliveries and Crockpot terms.

The big gimmick today is to find a recessionproof business—like predicting recessions.

Bankruptcy is when you're entitled to early retirement but the company beats you to it.

A business slowdown is the pause that depresses.

There is one great lesson to be learned in the world of business: when it comes to sticking out your neck—don't be a mole, but don't be a giraffe either.

The way to survive in either business or government is to be a firm believer in human rights. If any human over you says something, you say, "Right!"

Never lose sight of the first law of getting ahead in business: IT ISN'T WHAT YOU SNOW—IT'S WHO YOU SNOW!

There is only one problem with owning your own business. Your favorite flavor gets to be aspirin.

The nice part about being in business for yourself is that you can write off so many things—like your free time.

The biggest problem in the business world today is explaining to your wife a payroll that reads: Betty Jones, Peggy Smith, Susan White, Ruth Brown, and Hotlips Boomboom.

Then there's the sign at the Better Business Bureau: THE STUCK STOPS HERE.

The business world consists of the big shots, the little shots, the cheap shots, and the half shot. No wonder, at lunchtime, so many go out and get loaded.

There are certain things that tax your credibility—like the fourth anniversary of a going-out-of-business sale.

It's the sort of contract that doesn't fill you with confidence. For instance, it was witnessed by a notary private.

A kickback is where the giver says, "Thank you," and the recipient says, "Don't mention it!"

I think kickbacks ought to continue, providing the backs are kicked long enough, hard enough, and low enough.

CALIFORNIA

You really have to be impressed with California. This is the only state where they run "Benny Hill" as a documentary.

I love California. Where else can you see so many people sitting beside their swimming pools talking about conserving water?

It's amazing how tan everybody is in California. You're never quite sure if it's the sun or they're mainlining shoe polish.

The ultimate in rejection is a Californian saying you're too far out. This is the only state where you can see people sitting in cars, snapping their fingers to turn signals.

In California, the ultimate in rejection is when you go to a muscle beach and don't measure up—or a nude beach and don't measure down.

A lot of immature people live in Hollywood. You can tell. Hollywood is the only place I know where the Baskin-Robbins Flavor-of-the-Month is Thumb!

Do you realize that people in California own 9 million hair dryers? And that's not counting the women.

There's a new sect in San Francisco with a very interesting approach. They say that when you die you don't go to hell, you go to Los Angeles.

Los Angeles is a wonderful location for a political convention. If you want a smoke-filled room, all you have to do is open a window!

I like the approach of that group in California who want to pool their savings, buy all of the potting soil in Sears, and start their own country.

California is a great place for houses. California is where people who live in $600,000 houses don't take the morning paper. And you know why? The paper you have to pay cash for!

In California, couples who get a divorce play Community Property Monopoly. He lives in a hotel and she gets the house!

Community property is a quaint local custom where the husband takes the high road and his wife takes everything else!

California has had so much rain, it's the first time anyone was ever mugged for their canoe!

The big problem out West is mudslides. For the first time in years, Californians are going 55 miles an hour—but it's in houses.

I once asked a resident of San Francisco if he ever worried about earthquakes. He said his attitude could be summed up by a line from the song "It Had to Be You." I said, "What line is that?" He said, " 'With all your faults—I love you still.' "

The first real sign of an earthquake is when you can go surfing in your bathtub.

What can you really say about that last earthquake in California? I've heard of jiggle shows, but this is ridiculous!

CAMPAIGN PROMISES

It's ten o'clock. President (INCUMBENT), do you know where your campaign promises are?

Here are a few more late-breaking items: campaign promises.

When it comes to keeping his campaign promises, one politician has wrestled with his conscience. His conscience has now asked for two out of three falls.

I try never to feel superior to politicians. I figure their campaign promises have just as much longevity as my New Year's resolutions.

CAMPING

Camping is great for people who want to give up smoking, because it gives you something to do with your hands—scratch.

That's the one thing campers have to get used to—bites. The campground puts the bite on you. The general store puts the bite on you. The guides put the bite on you.

They said this campground has all modern facilities and they didn't lie. It's the first time I ever saw a bush that flushed.

When you consider what's being done with their land, wild flowers have every right to be.

The balance of nature has worked for millions of years. Let's not put our thumb on the scale.

CARS (NEW)

Before we begin, I have a special request from the car parker. Would the owner of the convertible with the pink fenders, tutti-frutti body, feather-boa hood ornament, and red satin seat covers please report to the parking lot? There's nothing wrong. He just wants to see what you look like.

A typical American is someone who buys a car for its clean, sleek lines—and then puts a ski rack in back and 500 pounds of camping equipment on top.

I know this sounds paranoid, but every time I buy a new car I get the feeling it's the one that was on the assembly line when everybody went out on strike—and when they got back, nobody could remember where they had left off.

I love that expression "Teddy Roosevelt and his Rough Riders." He must have bought his cars from the same dealer I do.

C.B. radios don't make sense. I know a fella who spends three hours a day talking to total strangers and doesn't even say, "Good morning," to his wife.

CARS (PRICES)

Is it true that when you pay list price for a new car the dealer toasts you with a special drink: a Screwed Driver?

Have you seen the prices of the new cars? Be honest now. Did you ever expect to pay $12,000 for anything that didn't come with a lawn?

There's only one thing that's keeping me from buying a 1985 car—a 1938 bankroll.

It's ridiculous how expensive modern packaging has become. Do you realize the average American buys $10 worth of gas and has to take it home in a $10,000 container?

All my life I've had my heart set on a Porsche—and the way things are going, I think that's the only part of me that's ever going to set on one.

CARS (SMALL)

The problem with a car that can get 39 miles on a gallon is, it tends to be a little underpowered. For instance, you have to put it in low to get off a candy wrapper.

These subcompact cars are definitely the answer to the energy problem. You read about them and take the bus.

Now I know why dealers stand behind every car they sell. They're afraid to get inside.

I wasn't really worried until I took a look at the heater. It's a hair dryer.

And they've made the tape deck standard equipment. It plays "Nearer, My God, to Thee."

CEMETERIES

We live in a society that is always trying to take the sting out of reality. For instance, we no longer call it a graveyard. It's a Home for the Terminally Still.

I know it sounds macabre, but have you priced cemetery plots lately? They're not so much a plot as a conspiracy.

You pay $500 for a plot but they do give you some extras—perpetual care, a twenty-four-hour chapel, a doorman, security, and an answering service.

I happen to be the suspicious type. For instance, I've always felt that reincarnation is just a sneaky way to sell more tombstones.

I love those tombstones that say GONE BUT NOT FORGOTTEN—and you have to pull aside the weeds to read them. . . . Now when I go, I *know* I'm not going to be forgotten. I bought the cemetery plot on time.

CHEERLEADERS

There's no question about it, there is too much violence in football. Every time I say something about the cheerleaders, my wife pokes me in the ribs.

I finally came up with a way to cope with the cheerleader problem. Whenever my wife asks me what's so great about our local football team, I say, "The tight ends." Let her figure out which ones.

The football season began in a rather spectacular way. The top of one of the cheerleader's costumes fell down. Then 80,000 people stood up and sang, " 'Oh, say, can you see?' "

I won't say how their costumes are cut but, from the front, the cheerleaders look like Dolly Parton. And from the back—they look like Dolly Parton, too.

CHILDREN

Birthdays are our opportunity to give to kids all of the things they have given to us—but how do you gift-wrap high blood pressure?

It's very depressing the first time you realize you have a cat that answers to "Kitty," a dog that answers to "Rover," and three kids who answer to nobody.

It's very hard to get kids to appreciate the things they have—like air conditioning. How do you say to a kid that somewhere in India there are children who are sweating?

They say the best time to shop for food is when you're not hungry. That's why I can never take the kids.

Thanks to the thrift, self-sacrifice, ambition, and the determination of parents to create an easier, trouble-free life for their families, today millions of kids have what their fathers and mothers never had—apathy.

It's all in the way you look at it. Some people say the new generation is still trying to find itself. The rest just say, "I have seen the future—and it shirks!"

The more I see of kids, the more I'm coming to the conclusion I was never their age.

Remember when kids were belted and tires weren't?

Kids today are very concerned with "finding themselves" and so were we. If we wanted to find ourselves at the dinner table, we went out and got a job.

It's always fascinating watching a group of young kids playing with toys. It's like taking a crash course in Remedial Greed.

You learn a lot about reality from your kids. One of them just bought a T-shirt that says THE BEST THINGS IN LIFE ARE FREE. It cost $4.98.

Now there's a new group consisting of couples with kids who are respectful, studious, intelligent, neat, and ambitious. It's called the P.L.O.—Parents Lucking Out!

Kids today have really been influenced by modern technology. I took my six-year-old to the circus and, as we walked in, we heard music. To me, it sounded like a steam calliope. To him, it sounded like dialing long distance.

We keep telling our kids they should have the wisdom to accept those things they cannot change—but one of them shouldn't be socks.

I won't say our kids are out of shape, but last Saturday our ten-year-old was panting and he was only in the game five minutes—and this was checkers.

A journey of a thousand miles begins with but a single step. It's usually taken by the five-year-old going back to use the bathroom.

CHILDREN'S CAMPS

Pretty soon millions of kids will be coming home from summer camp and so we should all relish our present condition: Terminal Quiet.

Our kids aren't thrilled with summer camp. In fact, one of them has run away from so many summer camps, we don't sew name tapes in his clothes—we sew road maps.

Kids always start off hating summer camp but then they are struck by the sudden realization of how great it all is. This sudden realization usually occurs in October.

I'm getting a little concerned about where my kids spent the summer. They said the owner had a little black mustache and he called the place Mein Kamp.

It's really a thrill when our kids come home from summer camp. We yell, "Eureka! Eureka!" And they really do. They haven't had a bath for weeks!

It's amazing. Yesterday our twelve-year-old came home from camp with a six-week accumulation of dirty laundry. What makes it so amazing—it was a three-week camp.

The kids got home from camp with a summer's worth of dirty laundry—which can be kind of embarrassing. How many people call Roto-Rooter for a washing machine?

CHINA

China offers fantastic opportunities for trade. The United States has 200 million bushels of corn, wheat, and soybeans—and China has 900 million cubic feet of stomach.

China has almost one billion people and there's a reason for this. When there's soft music, a bottle of wine and the lights are turned low—it's very hard to tell the difference between a bow and a nod.

The State Department has a program to condition diplomats to living in a country with one billion people. For starters, you move into a disco.

CHRISTMAS

Sometimes kids get very confused about Christmas. Like one little kid asked his mother, "Is it true that Santa Claus brings us presents?" She said, "Yes, that's true." He said, "And the stork brings us babies?" She said, "Yes, that's true." He said, "And the Police Department protects us?" She said, "That's right." He looked up at her and said, "Then what do we need Daddy for?"

It takes three kinds of people to make a Christmas: kids to ooh, mothers to ah, and fathers to owe.

I'll never forget the Christmas I spent in a nudist camp. It's the first time I ever heard it sung: "Stark, the Herald Angels Sing."

Have you ever noticed the relationship between Handel's "Messiah" and Congress? I'm serious. Every year, the minute Congress stops what they're doing and goes home for Christmas, choirs all over America start singing: "Hallelujah! Hallelujah! Hallelujah!"

Some people are so insensitive. Every Christmas my church asks me to be in the Hallelujah Chorus—and they know I don't dance.

If you've ever heard an amateur choir do it, you know why it's called the Hallelujah Chorus. When it ends, that's what you say.

One church is doing an updated version of the Christmas story. Instead of gold, frankincense, and myrrh—the three kings bring gold, investment diamonds, and the deed to a condominium in Florida.

Every time I hear the Christmas story of the infant Jesus born in a manger, I can't help but wonder if Mary and Joseph didn't have the same medical plan I do.

" 'Twas the night before Christmas and all through the house, not a creature was stirring, not even a mouse.' " Orkin strikes again!

We have sort of a Christmas tradition in our house. On Christmas Eve the kids all hang their socks over the fireplace, and when they're sound asleep we do something very unusual with their socks. We wash them.

Where else but in America could you buy a plastic tree with Styrofoam snow and electric candles to get that genuine Christmas feeling?

We were a lot better off when our Christmas spirit came by the heartful rather than the snootful.

CHRISTMAS CARDS

Each year as we stamp and address them,
And into each envelope stuff,
At Christmas the very best card trick—
Is simply just having enough.

It's amazing how irritated and grumpy you can get inserting, sealing, stamping, addressing, and mailing 300 cards wishing goodwill to all men.

You can always tell the Christmas card going to your boss. It's the one that costs more than the postage.

At least you have to give the post office credit for knowing when to quit. One of my Christmas cards came back with the notation: ADDRESSEE DECEASED. DO NOT FORWARD.

My wife always accuses me of being a procrastinator, so this morning I made it a point to finish addressing all of our Christmas cards —and in the spirit of the verse printed on them, let me wish you all a Merry Christmas and a very happy 1956.

CHRISTMAS GIFTS

Christmas is only three months away. I know Christmas is only three months away. I just heard a clerk rehearsing, "Batteries not included."

Sign in a gift shop window: HO HO HO SPOKEN HERE.

Talk about the Christmas spirit—our local finance company is giving out little bottles of cologne to all its customers—Eau de Owe.

I'll never forget this Christmas. The kids gave me after-shave lotion; my wife gave me a man's cologne; and the relatives gave me scented soap. It was a day of reekoning!

Nothing is ever wasted. The Christmas presents of today are the garage sales of tomorrow.

My kids are always caught on the horns of a moral dilemma at Christmastime: what do you give to a father who has everything— and they're using it?

I still haven't recovered from Christmas morning. There was this big pile of boxes and one read: OPEN ME FIRST. So I opened it first and it was the bills for all the rest.

Be honest now. If it wasn't for Christmas, how would you ever get to know your wife's sizes?

My nephew isn't too swift. Last year I gave him a $20 bill for Christmas. He asked if it came with batteries.

Voters have a terrible problem at Christmastime. What do you give to a politician who has everything—and half of it's yours?

They have some very unusual gifts this Christmas. For people who are always putting their foot in their mouth—Adidas mouthwash!

You know why instant cameras are so popular at Christmas? It's the only way you can get a picture of your child playing with an unbroken toy.

It's a good thing Christmas comes in December instead of July. Parking lot attendants would all be suffering from a very painful condition—sunburned palms.

CHRISTMAS (SANTA CLAUS)

Our kids have reached the age where they're beginning to get suspicious about Santa Claus. This morning one of them asked me how he could get all those millions and millions of different things into one bag. I said, "You ever look in your mother's purse?"

One of the first things parents learn at Christmastime is—the store may be discount but Santa's promises aren't.

Kids don't believe in things like Santa Claus and the Easter Bunny anymore. You mention the Tooth Fairy and they think you're talking about a dentist in San Francisco.

I'll tell you why I don't believe in Santa Claus. I can accept going around the entire world in one night bringing toys and goodies to every little boy and girl. What I can't accept is finding those 800 million parking places.

Nowadays, when you hear someone going, "Ho! Ho! Ho!"—do you ever get the feeling it was prerecorded in 1955?

Santa Claus is the one who's making a list and checking it twice—he's gonna find out who's naughty and nice. So are voters.

The last company I put money into went broke and I still don't know why. They made Santa Claus outfits in decorator colors.

CHRISTMAS SHOPPING

Consumers are shlock absorbers.

Christmas shopping time is here—when millions of Americans are on the verge of an urge to splurge!

My wife is shopping for Christmas gifts,
With purchases little and large;
She doesn't believe in Santa Claus—
But she sure does in Master Charge!

My wife left to go shopping at nine this morning. Here it is eight in the evening. She's not back and I'm really getting worried. I figure one of two things has happened. Either she's gone for the bundle or Macy's has taken hostages.

Maybe I'm just sentimental, but it brings tears to my eyes to see my loved ones leave home—along with my loved fives, my loved tens, and my loved twenties.

A fella down the street was putting on knee protectors, shin guards, shoulder pads, and a helmet. He said, "It's that time of the year again." I said, "Football? Playing?" He said, "Christmas. Shopping."

I've often wondered what people who work in department stores think about with the crowds and confusion and endless Christmas music and now I know. Last night I asked a clerk if they were going to close soon. She said, "No. It's only three 'Silent Nights' after five."

Last night I paid $39.95 for a doormat made of reindeer fur that plays "Santa Claus Is Coming to Town" when you stand on it. It's just amazing the things you do when you're under the influence of ho ho ho.

And Christmas is when the stores all hold these marvelous sales. I saw one item marked down $5.00. It was a Rolls-Royce.

Some businessmen are saying this could be the greatest Christmas ever. How do you like that? I always thought the first one was.

CHRISTMAS TOYS

We were in a big downtown department store when suddenly I started to pull my wife in one direction. She said, "Where are you going?" I said, "I want to visit Toyland." My wife just shook her head. She said, "You can't. Your passport has expired."

My kids are so lazy, for Christmas I had to give them prebroken toys.

Christmas is when parents wrap a toy machine gun in paper that says: PEACE ON EARTH. GOODWILL TO MEN.

Have you seen that doll that wets and then gets diaper rash? It prepares kids for what they'll want to be as adults—celibate.

We got our five-year-old a doll that wets and it's really confused the dog. All day long he sits in a corner thinking, "And me they hit with a newspaper!"

This year the accent is on realistic toys. For instance, there's a teenager doll. You wind it up and it resents you for it.

Did you hear about the kid who got the most realistic present of all? All he wanted for Christmas was a passenger train—and it never showed up.

This year they have something really new for Christmas—a toy-operated battery!

Misery on Christmas morning is a kid with six new toys and twelve old batteries.

Batteries are now so much a part of Christmas, you can't blame kids for being confused. They think we're celebrating the birth of Eveready!

'Twas the month after Christmas, and all through the house, not a game there was stirring. Dead batteries!

CHRISTMAS TREES

I have a great idea for keeping Christmas trees year after year. Leave them in the forest.

> We always get a natural tree.
> There's something about them that's nice:
> Real scent, real needles, real branches, real trunk.
> All that's unreal is the price!

Have you noticed how rare green Christmas trees have become? They're either red or silver or gold or blue. Like, where is Grecian Formula when we really need it?

You have to feel sorry for Christmas trees. We bring them into our homes, we put them in the biggest rooms, we dress them up with lights and ornaments, we sprinkle them with silver, and we invite all the neighbors in to share their glory. Then, two weeks later, they're all in garbage trucks saying, "What did I do wrong?"

CITIES

The art museum in my hometown just acquired an early Rembrandt. A very early Rembrandt. It's done in Crayola.

I come from one of those cities that has a master plan for the downtown area. It's called neglect.

No wonder so many cities are losing the ball game. They have their tax base too far from home.

What can you really say about (DEPRESSED URBAN AREA)? I didn't even know Edsel made cities.

Is it true, if you say to someone, "Where in hell have you been?"— they start telling you about (PROBLEM-PLAGUED CITY).

Big-city airports and big-city bus terminals have an entirely different approach to the problems of transportation. The airports are located twenty miles outside of the city and it takes you an hour to get downtown. On the other hand, bus terminals are located right in the heart of the city—in a neighborhood where it takes you an hour to get up the courage to leave.

We live in a lovely little suburb. It's just two miles beyond our income.

I'm always intrigued by the way cities cope with snowstorms. First the snowplow comes through and pushes the snow off to the side. Then homeowners shovel it out in the center again. Four hours later the snowplow comes through and pushes it off to the side. Then homeowners shovel it out to the center again. The next day the snowplow comes through and pushes it off to the side. Then homeowners shovel it out to the center again. We don't really remove snow. We nag it to death!

CIVILIZATION

Civilization is when people who live in Alaska burn oil to produce electricity to run refrigerators to keep food cold.

What a wonderful world this could have been if Eve had just found a no-fault apple.

We're living in an age that places great demands on people. Frankly, I don't know that I'm up to remembering my Social Security number, my mantra, and my C.B. call name—all at the same time.

What can I tell you? Nowadays you don't have to be a belly dancer to have the shakes!

When it comes to achievement, we really should give more credit to our Stone Age ancestors. Do you realize what cunning and strength it took to hunt dinosaurs? The decoy alone weighed three tons!

CLOSINGS

As any audience knows, there is no better painkiller than "Thank you and good night."

ENDING A VERY LONG MEETING: The Bible tells us, "Blessed are the merciful." This meeting is now adjourned.

CLOSING A LONG MEETING: I have always believed that a word to the wise is sufficient. It is now midnight and the word is: Adjourned!

CLOSING A PANEL DISCUSSION: It's ten o'clock and I'm afraid it's time to put a silencer on our big guns.

In conclusion, a finished speaker knows when to finish speaking. Thank you and good night.

In conclusion, let me end this session with one sobering thought: it's ten o'clock. Do you know where your Treasurer is?

In bringing this speech to an end, I have always believed that actions speak louder than words. (AND THEN GO BACK TO YOUR SEAT.)

And now, as one schizophrenic said to the other, "Let's split!"

CONCLUDING A ROAST: First, I would like to ask you all to join me in a moment of silence for all the reputations that have died here tonight.

As we learned tonight, there is no substitute for a good speech—so next week we're going to try again.

CLOTHING

Permanent press is a marvelous thing.
It eliminates much fuss;
But nowadays, with inflation—
What's permanently pressed is us!

DRY CLEANERS HIT THE SPOT!

People are becoming more and more fashion conscious. You've heard of the KKK? They're now wearing designer sheets.

It's very revealing how a country uses see-through fabrics. In America, they're used for blouses. In Russia, for voting booths.

I like that coat. It's the first time I ever saw a double-knit mink.

The messages on T-shirts are getting much more elaborate. Phyllis Diller wears one that has the Golden Rule. Bo Derek wears one that has the Gettysburg Address. And Dolly Parton wears one that has the first three volumes of the Encyclopedia Britannica.

My wife has come to the reluctant conclusion that when they say, "ONE SIZE FITS ALL"—they're talking about Sybil All, who's a perfect 36.

You should have seen this bathing suit. It looked like something three silkworms turned out on their coffee break!

Clothing stores are trying to find a name for those short shorts women are wearing. How about Breeches of Promise?

But if women want to wear those real short shorts—I'm behind them all the way!

The women in our neighborhood are a little upset because the girl next door is wearing a twenty-inch slit skirt. They're upset for three reasons: she's young, she's pretty, and she's a midget.

If men really wanted women who are prudent, practical, economical, and down-to-earth—there would be a much bigger market for double-knit negligees.

I didn't know long johns were underwear. I thought long johns were the fellas who posed for *Playgirl*.

There are so many mysteries in life—like, why do they call them Jockey shorts when it's the other kind that ride up?

Yesterday I opened the closet to take out my winter clothes and right away I knew I was in trouble. Three moths flew out and one was a Cuban adviser.

In colonial times, men wore wigs, ruffled shirts, tight-fitting satin pants, and silk stockings. In those days (LOCAL MEN'S STORE) looked just like your wife's closet.

To save a little money, I've been buying clothes through the mail and it's really great. You send them your measurements and two weeks later you get a suit that makes you look like a famous person in literature—Quasimodo.

One time they sent me a pair of slacks with thirty-two-inch legs and a twenty-two-inch zipper. It didn't do much for my appearance but my social life is booming.

COFFEE

I tried to give up coffee in the morning but the first thing I noticed when I woke up is I didn't.

There is no real substitute for coffee or what coffee can do for you. I mean, who ever heard of tomato juice nerves?

Coffee also does interesting things to your breath. I know a fella who drinks twelve cups of coffee and smokes three packs of cigarettes a day and it's amazing. This morning he exhaled and three flowers on his breakfast table died. What makes it so amazing, they were plastic.

I won't say what coffee breath is like but after three cups you have to file an environmental impact statement.

Have you noticed how restaurants are trying to economize on coffee? I ordered a cup at our local diner, looked at it, called the owner over and said, "Pete, want to know how to sell twice as much coffee as you're now selling?" He said, "Sure." I said, "Fill the cups!"

Some restaurants are charging $1.50 for a cup of coffee. Be honest now, did you ever expect to spend $1.50 to drink something that didn't come with an olive?

Remember when we used to discuss our problems over a cup of coffee? Now coffee is one of the problems.

COLLEGE

College Board test scores have been declining for many years. One campus has its own memorial—the Tomb of the Unknown Answer.

Thanks to truth in advertising, it will no longer be called "college." It will be called "remedial high school."

If you're filthy rich, sending your kids to college makes a wonderful soap.

Our neighbor asked us how it feels to have a daughter in college. I said it's like a quotation from the Good Book: "And a little child shall bleed them!"

We have a daughter who's two months into her freshman year. Judging from her phone calls, I think she's majoring in Panic.

And the courses she's taking. One is called "An Introduction to the Cinema." For those of you not familiar with "An Introduction to the Cinema"—it's when your kids pay a hundred dollars a point to see the same movies you saw at twenty-five cents on Saturday night. . . . They get a degree and you got dishes.

Our son in college must really be having trouble with parcel post. Last week he tried to telegraph home his laundry.

I won't say what his laundry is like, but as a wedding present we were given a pair of sterling silver serving tongs—and for many years we used them in the dining room so that our hands would never have to touch the food. Now we use them in the laundry room so that our hands won't ever have to touch his socks.

But after they're washed, they do come out smelling like the great outdoors—particularly if you live in Pittsburgh.

Why is it that colleges never give practical courses, like Laundromat 101? . . . You know how France has vintage wines? Our son comes home with vintage laundry. . . . I want to tell you something—1984 was not a good year for socks!

We spent $5000 sending him to a speech therapist because he talks through his nose. Then we found out why. With his laundry, he doesn't want to smell through it!

And it's always a shock when your kids come home from college. You get the feeling that what they majored in was Hunger.

Even as a kid I was skinny. When I was ready to go to college, my family had to send me to Iowa. It was the only school whose letter fit my chest.

Palimony settlements have set a lot of people thinking. I know two college kids who are trying to work up a living-together financial agreement—but it's run into a snag. They can't decide who gets custody of the Twinkies.

COLLEGE GRADUATES

My nephew, the college graduate, is really astute. When we were in Washington he saw the original of the Declaration of Independence and he said that, just by looking at it, you could tell it was very important. I said, "How is that?" He said, "The whole thing is written in italics."

If you put your son through four years of college and now he's a beachcomber, the B.A. he got stands for Benedict Arnold.

I watched the kid next door go through four years of football games, cultural enrichment programs, basketball games, overseas study trips, band practice, a wilderness survival course, not to mention remedial English, math, and science—and today he finally graduated with a B.S. degree. He asked me if I knew what the B.S. stood for. Needless to say, my first guess was wrong.

When our son said he wanted to go to college, we had a party and served something appropriate—imported champagne. When he said he wanted to go on to get his master's, we had a party and served something appropriate—domestic champagne. Yesterday he said he wanted to go on to get his Ph.D. and we still had a party and served something appropriate—sponge cake.

Every year American colleges and universities graduate a few million liberal arts majors and it's really upgrading our way of life. You don't know what a thrill it is to see your kid filling out an unemployment form in Latin.

The best degrees are the ones in specific areas—like psychology, engineering, business administration. At least you know what kind of work you're out of.

COLLEGE SPORTS

College football is a game that instills a sense of fair play and good sportsmanship—in everybody but the alumni.

> I love to watch college football.
> Still a question persists as I look:
> I know they can go through a line—
> But when have they gone through a book?

I don't really mind when athletes who are classified as amateur go to college and get free tuition, free room and board, free books, free laundry, and free medical care. What bothers me is when they major in ethics.

I went to one of those colleges where they burned the football coach in effigy—and everything else in the cafeteria.

I went to a very small college. Very small. You know how some colleges have marching bands? We had a marching trio.

For those of you who have never heard a college marching band, it's 142 students each hoping the others can play.

Did you ever get the feeling that, with some colleges, their team ought to march and their band ought to play?

COLUMBUS

We owe a lot to Christopher Columbus. If it wasn't for Columbus, the capital of Ohio would be known as   .

Columbus is the one who wanted to go to India and wound up in San Salvador. I've had travel agents like that myself.

Columbus is the one who came ashore and said, "I claim this land for the King and Queen of Spain"—and it really surprised the Indians because they didn't even know they had it listed.

America continues to be the great melting pot. When before have you ever heard a name like Bobbie Sue Wong?

That's the big thing these days—double names. Bobbie Sue, Billy Bob, Glory Bea, Baba Rhum! . . . Nowadays you don't say a name. You snap your fingers to it.

COMMITTEES

The thing to be wary of, when serving on a committee, is the can-do spirit. Because the minute you say you can, the others respond with, "Do!"

A fund-raising committee is a group of people who get together to get—together.

The minority report on a committee is most likely to be turned in by the member least likely to benefit from the majority report.

If you're the Program Chairman of a club, the most important thing is to be able to speak on your feet. Which isn't easy, because if you've allowed yourself to become Program Chairman of a club, that's where your brains are.

The Treasurer has asked me to invite you all to become members of our Ad Hoc Journal Committee—because if we don't sell more ads, we're never going to get out of hock!

You can always tell if a speaker is lying by looking into his eyes. (PUT ON A PAIR OF SUNGLASSES.) And so, as I begin this Treasurer's Report—

Sitting at the head table does a little for your ego—but a lot for your table manners.

COMPUTERS

I'll tell you what kind of an office I work in. We have a computer with ulcers.

Our boss has a very simple attitude toward automation. He'll try it when they come up with a computer that cringes.

Automation is when you need seven machines to replace the one office boy who used to go out for coffee, Cokes, sandwiches, potato chips, ice cream, candy, and cigarettes.

I don't like the ads they're running on that new office machine. They claim it can do the work of three executives—or one secretary.

I know a couple who met each other through one of those computer matching services and it really works. He manufactures doorbells and she's a ding-a-ling!

Some people think that modern life is too impersonal and that we're all being reduced to faceless components in a computerized society. Well, I don't agree—and neither does my wife, 602-33-5968.

Everything balances out. Computers have saved the millions and millions of man-hours we now need to straighten out all the mistakes in computer billing.

Computer experts now think in terms of microseconds. For those of you not familiar with a microsecond, it's the amount of time that elapses between the receipt of your degree and the first solicitation from the Alumni Fund.

CONGRESS

Sometimes I get the feeling that Congress really doesn't grasp the enormity of our problems. That, if they had been around in Noah's time, they would have been stockpiling Totes.

We have detergents, soap powders, cold remedies, and headache pills that are faster acting. Now if we could only have a Congress.

Purgatory is a place of great confusion where the inhabitants aren't sure if they're going to heaven or hell. We have the same thing here in Washington. It's called Congress.

Last week the eastern part of the United States was once again confronted by a devastating seasonal phenomenon—an incredible wind going around in circles. Meteorologists call it—Congress.

Congress is back in session again. If you were unkind, you might call it their second wind.

In all fairness, it isn't easy sitting in the Congress day after day. It's like having Howard Cosell for a roommate.

Our forefathers wanted us to have representative government in the worst possible way—and every time I look at Congress, I think we do.

The Congress is going all out for truth and honesty in everything it does. For instance, the Congressional Record is now being sent as junk mail.

Have you ever read the Congressional Record? It's almost like a religious experience: it passeth all understanding.

Did you ever get to wondering what Congress did before confusion was invented?

Is it true that if God had been a congressman He would have rested on the first, fifth, sixth, and seventh days?

I won't say how much activity the Congress has shown this year but it's the only place in America where self-winding watches don't.

I won't say what it's accomplished, but this could be the first Congress ever arrested for loitering.

The problem in government isn't so much nonessential spending as nonessential spenders.

Do you ever get to wondering what Congress does for a living?

If absence makes the heart grow fonder, a lot of congressmen must really love their job!

The voters back home are worried about our congressman's appearance. He hasn't made one in six months.

I'd like to say something good about America: Congress has now gone home. Good!

The Congress is in recess again. It's almost as if Johnny Carson is catching.

The Congress has gone home. Some people call it an adjournment. Some refer to it as Congress Interruptus.

Some call it "going home." Others—"returning from the scene of the crime."

And you have to admire the calm, thoughtful, reasoned manner in which the Congress ended this session. It was done in a way that was reminiscent of the best efforts of three other great Americans —Groucho, Chico, and Harpo.

It's fascinating the way Congress always weasels on its pay raises. Believe me, there's more to this organization than meets the nose.

Congressmen are now earning $69,800. It's ridiculous. Why, I know doctors who don't make that in a week!

Our congressman is a little on the sentimental side. He had a framed bill on the wall of his office. It's the first dollar he ever taxed.

I get very envious of congressmen who are only twenty-eight years old. I have loans that are older than that.

Congress has been called the greatest deliberative body in the world. Not so. (SEX SYMBOL) is the greatest deliberative body in the world. Our office alone has spent hours deliberating on it.

CONVENTIONS

Energy conservation has had a profound effect on conventions. What used to be shirt-sleeve sessions are now cardigan conferences.

I'll tell you what kind of a year we've had. Last week I went to a convention under an assumed name tag.

It's just wonderful to see the preparations the hotel has made for this convention. It's the first time I ever saw a Gideon Bible on a chain.

CORRUPTION

It's very important to get the terminology in all this correct. First, there's the operation that catches the crooked politicians. This is called The Sting. Then there are the people who voted for the politicians. These are called The Stung.

There are subtle little signs when politicians are on the take. Little things, like being able to say, "For me?" in twenty-six different languages.

Now, in Florida, things are different. In Florida, it's a cinch to spot politicians who are on the take. Their palms are sunburned.

But I think it's time we showed a little tolerance. For instance, let's not call them crooked politicians. I mean, if you had $50,000 in one pocket, you'd tilt too.

I don't know about you, but if I carried $50,000 around in my pocket, I'd get all my pants from Brink's.

It's going to be very interesting to see what happens to these politicians. I understand the Ethics Committee is already working on a group tch-tch.

We're beginning to hear a lot about entrapment. For those of you who aren't familiar with the concept—entrapment is when you settle down to read and your wife offers you two magazines: *Family Circle* and *Playboy*.

What we really need is a slogan to encourage politicians to stay honest. Something like: MAKE LAWS, NOT LICENSE PLATES!

COSMETICS

Have you noticed how cosmetic companies list the ingredients in their products in the order of their importance? For instance, first there's profit.

Women now know exactly what is in the cosmetics they're using. When a husband says, "Dear, what makes your skin so soft, so supple, so enticing, so alluring?"—with total confidence they can answer, "Goose grease!"

Can you imagine having to list all of the chemicals that go into cosmetics? The most popular new perfume could be MIDNIGHT IN DU PONT.

Things like perfumes and colognes and deodorants are becoming increasingly important because kids don't take as many baths these days. One kid came home from college, walked into the kitchen, and said to his mother, "Is that dinner I smell?" She said, "It is and you do."

CREDIT

I admire the way my wife spends. She's a credit to her card.

Credit Crunch! What a great name for Baskin-Robbins Flavor-of-the-Month!

We deal with a very effective collection agency. Maybe you've heard of it—Attila the Dun!

CRIME

If voluntary compliance with the law worked, Moses would have come down from Mount Sinai with the Ten Guidelines.

The way things are going, we no longer need a good Samaritan. We need a great Samaritan.

This happens to be a very friendly town. If you want to shake hands with someone you must reach into your wallet pocket.

You think you have troubles. I was mugged on a roller coaster. Nobody noticed because I had my hands up!

If Bob Hope is planning to entertain our fighting forces this Christmas, I know a police station in (HIGH CRIME DISTRICT) that would love to have him.

City officials asked (WINNING CANDIDATE) not to respond to his victory by holding his hands above his head. There are too many people downtown doing that already.

Last night I heard someone trying to break into our house, so I picked up the biggest thing I could find—my mortgage payment.

We feel very secure in our home because there's nothing left to steal. We call it Attack Poverty!

Millions of American homes have electronic timers that automatically turn on the lights when no one is home—and it's really made an impact. For the first time in history, burglars don't have to use one hand to carry a flashlight.

I come from a very poor state. You know how some states have electric chairs? Ours had a windup!

You can always tell the states that coddle their criminals. They have electric recliners.

Nolo contendere is a legal term meaning, "I didn't do it, Judge, and I'll never do it again!"

Many a crooked scheme has been born on a legal pad.

I'm always a little suspicious of people who say: "As God is my witness." You're never sure if it's for the defense or the prosecution.

There is one great flaw in the trial-by-jury system. It's a little frightening to know that your fate is in the hands of twelve people who weren't smart enough to get excused.

CRUISES

We had a fantastic vacation last year. We bought a new car, put all the kids in the back seat, and took a cruise.

Cruises are very expensive. If you don't believe it, look at the Ship of State.

Noah's family sailed for forty days and forty nights and, when they left the ark, they kissed the ground. I've been on cruise ships like that myself.

Girls who take cruises soon discover that men fall into two categories—those who are on the level and those who are on the boat.

I had a terrible experience this week. I was hit by a cruise missile—the bill for my trip to the Caribbean.

CUBA

Who would have ever figured Cuba to become a military power? You ever try to march to "Babalu?"

Their crack unit is the 341st Mortar and Bongo Battalion.

We have to be very careful because, in all fairness, we sometimes make a charge that is only 50% correct. We call Castro a barefaced liar.

DALLAS

My favorite television show is "Dallas." I won't say what goes on in this show but the scripts are written on plain brown wrappers.

It's really steamy. We were watching one scene and my wife said, "Well, I never!"—while they were.

It's kinda hard to describe how one character spends her time, but last week she came down with a very strange ailment—an ingrown mattress.

She has only one disappointment in life and that's with Texas men. They're all six-footers—but not where it counts.

She's what you might call a demure girl. That's why if you date her there's good news and bad news. The bad news is, she only entertains gentleman callers in the parlor. The good news is, it's the massage parlor.

And "Dallas" is a show that isn't afraid to explore controversial subjects. Next week's story is all about a Texas minister who loses his faith. No longer believes in the Dallas Cowboys!

"Dallas" is all about a Texas family that's rich. Very rich. You can tell that in the opening scene as they all prepare to visit their local Rolls-Royce showroom—for its annual Mix or Match sale.

Lots of families have money but, with them, it's real money. For instance, they're the only ones I know who support a foster child in Beverly Hills. . . . Their gardener is an Arab.

This family has so much money, they had to take up speed reading just to get through their bankbooks.

They live on an estate called Southfork. Nobody really knows how far south this estate goes, but their house pets are three dogs, two cats, and a penguin.

DAUGHTERS

I come from a very practical town. Parents never worry about their daughters going out on a date providing their shoes are tied—to each other.

It's no wonder parents are confused. I have a daughter who has jeans that say CALVIN KLEIN, dresses that say CHRISTIAN DIOR, scarves that say VERA, shoes that say GUCCI, skirts that say PUCCI, purses that say YVES ST. LAURENT—and what does she keep telling us? "I want to be me!"

Our daughter just got married and I think it's going to be all right. She has that homemaking instinct. Yesterday she asked my wife to write down the recipe for a peanut butter and jelly sandwich.

DENTISTS

I'm always intrigued by that commercial where they talk about the kids getting a good report from the dentist. The only report I ever got from a dentist was that my check bounced.

I went to the dentist because I'm having trouble with my bite. I still want to.

Nowadays a million-dollar smile could mean inlays.

DESIGNER JEANS

My neighbor isn't speaking to me today. Yesterday she wore a pair of slacks with the name CALVIN KLEIN on the right side of the seat. I said, "And what do you call the other one?"

The big thing with designer jeans is, they're tight. Very tight. Very, very tight. One brand is so tight—sitting down in them automatically qualifies you for the Vienna Boys' Choir.

I went into a clothing store and I was told that the absolutely tightest pair of designer jeans sold is called EE-I-EE-I-O. I said to the clerk, "EE-I-EE-I-O? Because of the barnyard influence?" He said, "No. EE-I-EE-I-O—because of what you say when you put them on!"

Designer jeans are so tight, Zero Population Growth is even en-
couraging couples to get married in them. By the time they get
them off, they're divorced.

Designer jeans are so tight, you can't even call the fastener in front
a zipper. It's more like a do-it-yourself vasectomy.

If you've never seen designer jeans, picture what would happen if
Paris made Lubbock its sister city.

It doesn't make sense. The top designers in the world are vying
with each other to put their names on the back seats of jeans. I can
remember when you wanted to have your name on people's lips.

The good news is, we're living in a time when millions of Americans are finally beginning to turn the other cheek. The bad news is,
it's to show the designer label on their jeans.

They're called designer jeans—or, in the immortal words of the old
proverb, a fool and his money are soon tailored.

There are two things you should know about designer jeans. Because of the tailoring, you should never put anything in your
pocket. And because of the price, you *can* never put anything in
your pocket.

An ornithologist claimed there are now 40 million pigeons in the
United States. Thirty million are birds and the rest are people who
pay $40 for blue jeans.

Forty dollars! I can remember when blue jeans were clothes you
worked long hours in. Now they're clothes you work long hours
for.

DIETS

They say America is a melting pot. Now if we could only convince
dieters.

It's very discouraging. The kids are on a diet. My wife is on a diet. I'm on a diet. But the only thing in our house that's losing weight is the refrigerator.

The newest technique in dieting is to really lay it on the line. Put up a sign on your refrigerator door:

TO KEEP YOUR TUMMY YUMMY,
DON'T OVERLOAD IT, DUMMY!

> When dieting, avoid all sweets,
> No matter if they're yummy;
> They may melt inside your mouth—
> But they firm up on your tummy!

When dieting, never lose sight of the Won Ton Factor. If you eat all you Won, you're gonna weigh a Ton!

My mother was always dieting. To this day I think of a home-cooked meal as grapefruit and black coffee.

My wife is a perpetual dieter. If she had come down from Mount Sinai, the two tablets she carried would have been saccharin.

I'll never forget the first time I went on a diet. It was the same day I realized our bathtub was form-fitting.

I used to have 46-inch hips—so I started drinking low-fat milk. Now I have 46-inch knees.

I've been on a diet so long, yesterday someone gave me a cake fork and I asked if it came with instructions.

I just went on a fantastic new diet. You only eat at (LOSING CANDIDATE) victory parties.

I finally found a diet that works. You only eat when the weather is good.

Thanks to a diet book, I just dropped two pounds. Tossed it into the garbage.

Our neighbor lost twenty-two pounds and it's all because of the grapefruit diet. Every morning he goes down to the market and unloads 800 crates of grapefruit.

I happen to know there's a lot of fooling around at some of those diet clubs. It's not at all unusual for an unmarried couple to go upstairs, lock the door, and compare cellulite.

It's a heartrending sight to see the members of a diet club who fall off the wagon. One member showed up under the influence of chocolate cream pie. . . . Another OD'd on Twinkies.

DINNERS

Party politics is when you tell the hostess the dinner was great.

> The cocktail hour is ending,
> The salad is now being tossed;
> Please go to your table for dinner—
> He who hesitates is sauced!

Last night at dinner, Family Fight Number 2184 began. I cast my bread upon the waters. My wife said it was soup.

I'll never forget one of the first meals my wife ever made—roast pork—may it rest in grease.

I wish my wife wouldn't keep saying she's "fixing" dinner. It always makes me wonder what went wrong.

I don't think I could ever become a vegetarian. Who can sit down to candlelight, a glass of superb red wine, pick up a knife and fork —and then salivate over filet of soybean?

Southern cooking can be quite an experience. Yesterday I was given a plate of hog jowls, chitlins, and fatback—and I asked if it came with instructions!

DISCOS

I went to a discotheque on Wall Street and it was just fascinating. The most popular dance was called the Portfolio Shuffle.

There's a reason why it's called disco dancing. After two hours, every disc in your body is saying, "Oh!"

It's kinda hard to describe disco dancing. It's like having jock itch while standing in a bucket of cement.

You can always tell when you're overdoing the disco scene. It's when your shorts wear out from the inside.

And people wear the darnedest things in discos. I saw one girl wearing a pair of low-cut overalls. Looked like they came from Frederick's of Sioux City.

They say that disco music is so loud, it can damage ears. I say, "Don't worry. Anyone with an ear could never listen to that music."

Have you ever seen disco sheet music? It's four bars and then seven pages of ditto marks.

Discos are where people pay $50 a visit to hear sounds migraine sufferers pay $50 a visit to cure.

DOCTORS

Did you ever get the mad, uncontrollable urge to look in a faith healer's medicine chest?

Have you ever gone to a chiropractor? It's fascinating. Sounds as if your joints are eating Fritos.

I've lived a very sheltered life. I always thought a gynecologist was a person who's trying to protect gyns.

We're living in an age of medical specialists. Nowadays what four out of five doctors recommend is another doctor.

I like the spirit of the proctologist who escorts you to the door and says, "Don't worry. We'll have you on your seat in no time!"

My doctor told me it was disgraceful the way I was abusing my body by overeating. At least, I think that's what he said. With his smoker's cough, it's so hard to understand him.

I was once operated on by a twenty-three-year-old surgeon, and that's kinda scary. It's the first time I ever saw surgical mittens.

Every year it's the same thing. My doctor gives me something he says is good for hay fever. Just once I'd like to get something that's *bad* for hay fever!

More and more doctors are running their practices like an assembly line. One fella walked into a doctor's office and the receptionist asked him what he had. He said, "Shingles." So she took down his name, address, medical insurance number and told him to have a seat. Fifteen minutes later a nurse's aide came out and asked him what he had. He said, "Shingles." So she took down his height, weight, a complete medical history, and told him to wait in an examining room. A half hour later a nurse came in and asked him what he had. He said, "Shingles." So she gave him a blood test, a blood pressure test, an electrocardiogram, told him to take off all his clothes and wait for the doctor. An hour later the doctor came in and asked him what he had. He said, "Shingles." The doctor said, "Where?" He said, "Outside in the truck. Where do you want them?"

I know a doctor who's so independent, he won't even make hospital calls!

Now I know where the phrase "family doctor" comes from. For what he charges, you could raise a family.

I started getting a little suspicious of this doctor when he claimed I had an ingrown navel.

I think I know why doctors call it your annual checkup. Each year what goes up is your check.

It's a funny thing about doctors. When you try to make an appointment with a doctor, they float like a butterfly. But when you get their bill, they sting like a bee.

In all fairness, doctors do have a big investment in overhead and equipment. I know one doctor who had to trade in his adding machine for a newer model. It only went up to a million.

I saw a report that claims that a typical physician only made $65,000 last year. Unfortunately, this typical physician was driving his Rolls-Royce back to his twenty-two-room, six-acre estate and so was unable to comment on the accuracy of this report.

There's something wrong when a good funeral costs you $1500 and a good operation $5000.

Historians have now learned that there was a Declaration of Independence written in 1772—four years before Thomas Jefferson's Declaration of Independence. Only it was written by a doctor and nobody could read it.

DRINKING

I just figured out who originated that very romantic toast—where you drink champagne by looping your arm around the arm of your partner. Dry cleaners!

Eating will never solve as many problems as drinking. You ever try to tell your troubles to the busboy at a salad bar?

I don't care what is said about nonprescription drugs, I'm a firm believer in that product you take for the relief of occasional simple nervous tension—booze.

My wife doesn't drink and every year she asks: "What do I put in the eggnog?" I said: "Anything alcoholic." So she threw in her father.

> My wife drinks pop from aluminum cans,
> And I drink beer from them too;
> And when we return them I can't help but think:
> It's a recycle built for two!

My brother has gained a few pounds. I think he's aware of it. I just saw him drinking skimmed Pabst.

You can always tell the beer drinkers in any crowd from purple chests. It's from going (STIFLE A BURP WHILE TAPPING YOUR CHEST WITH THE SIDE OF YOUR FIST).

You can always tell the nouveaux riches. They're the ones who order Dom Perignon Lite.

Have you noticed all the new milk drinks with alcohol in them? No wonder those cows are contented!

I dunno. It just seems wrong to mix alcohol with milk. Somehow I just can't picture (MACHO TYPE) bellying up to the bar and saying, "Gimme a slug of Borden's!"

I don't mind trying to save money by buying unknown brands, but have you ever tried drinking Chivas Peasant?

Glasses make all women more desirable—martini glasses.

My idea of the quintessential dry martini is pouring straight gin into all the glasses—and then putting vermouth in the humidifier.

The best martini I ever tasted consisted of three parts gin and a vermouth-flavored stirrer.

It all comes down to a simple choice: there are many ways to become breathless. Some prefer running. Some prefer jogging. I prefer Smirnoff's.

To save money, always ask for a painkiller by its generic name— bourbon!

Life can be enormously satisfying once you learn one basic fact: a Water Pik also works with bourbon.

I'd be all for that idea to get fresh water by towing an iceberg down from the Arctic Circle—provided we could also tow up a bourbon factory from Tennessee.

If your nerves are shot, it doesn't help to reload with bourbon.

DRIVING

Something's got to be done about the pothole problem. Something dramatic—like getting every street in town to brush with Crest.

I live on a street with so many potholes, it looks like a pinball machine with curbs. . . . Any car with its wheels aligned is a tourist.

America is now faced with two major problems: deficits and the balance of payments—and potholes and the balance of pavements.

And it's always an adventure calling the Highway Department about a pothole. They said, "Exactly how deep is it?" I said, "How would I know?" They said, "Can't you look down?" I said, "No, I'm afraid of heights!"

I like the bumper sticker that reads: THIS IS AN UNMARKED CAR. PLEASE KEEP IT THAT WAY.

> Divided highways and limited exits
> Your mind can really blow.
> What they keep you divided from
> Is where you want to go.

I'd drive 55 miles per hour if it wasn't for the noise factor—all those other cars hitting your rear end.

Humor is a relative thing. To a child, humor is the circus clown. To a teenager, humor is the *National Lampoon*. And to a truck driver, humor is the 55-mile-an-hour speed limit.

I don't like driving on icy roads. There's something very disconcerting about your tires going 55 miles per hour but your car is backing up.

Icy roads are when your kids drive the way they always do—only now they have a reason for it.

> The temperature's far below zero,
> The roads are all covered with sleet;
> The car you can't start in the morning—
> Is the one you can't stop on the street.

He's not exactly a bad driver. Let's just say he's the only one I know with a black belt in parking.

DRUNKS

I just figured out why nobody gets drunk at sports events anymore. Who wants to see two Howard Cosells?

There is one sure way to tell if you're drinking too much. It's when you ask yourself, "What wine goes with bourbon?"

Two drunks were talking in a bar and one said, "I can still remember my wedding day. My wife had something old, something new, something borrowed, something blue!" The other drunk said, "What was blue?" He said, "Me. Her father had me by the throat!"

DRUNK: Ladies and gentlemen, I'd like to introduce my co-star—the tight at the end of the tunnel.

Sir, you've reached Alcoholic. Would you now like to try for Anonymous?

Sir, in a few minutes I'm going to take questions from the floor—and in a few minutes, something tells me that's where you're going to be.

Sir, the next time you have a train of thought, would you leave off the bar car?

Sir, is it true they named a forest after you—the Petrified?

ECONOMISTS

I wish government economists wouldn't keep saying they see the light at the end of the tunnel. It might just be a search party looking for survivors.

The last syllable of the word "economist" has always bothered me. Isn't "mist" another word for fog?

I've finally found one thing I have in common with my son. He listens to rock groups and I listen to economists—and neither one of us understands a word they're saying.

Have you noticed, there are very few thin economists? It's all those words they have to eat.

These are very difficult times for economists. In fact, the fastest-selling item on Wall Street today is a crystal ball in the Wharton School colors.

Do you ever get the feeling that tea-leaf readers are economists trying to better themselves?

Government economists are wondering what they can do about the leading economic indicators turning down. Well—there's always oysters.

Economists say there is no such thing as a free lunch. Now if we could only convince my brother-in-law.

I phoned an economist and asked if he could explain why American productivity is so low. He said, "I'll call you back after the coffee break."

ECONOMY

Communism is the system whereby everybody shares equally in getting the short end of the stick. Capitalism is the system that makes longer sticks.

I just ran across a bit of folk wisdom: you can always tell how cold the economic climate will be by studying the thickness of the heads in Washington.

I just read a fascinating classified ad. It said: FOR SALE. UNITED STATES TREASURY. TAKE OVER PAYMENTS.

I don't want to criticize the way the President is handling the economy, but I think they finally cloned Herbert Hoover.

I figured it out this morning,
Just what these words have meant;
In depressions you're really broke—
In recessions you're merely bent.

Prosperity is when people eat steak. Normalcy is when they eat hamburger. A recession is when they eat dog food. And a depression is when there isn't enough of it to go around.

I'll tell you what this year has been like. This is the first Thanksgiving dinner when we've ever had a turkey who volunteered.

Economizing is always a very delicate matter. Like the fella who does circumcisions, you have to be very careful where you cut.

A recession is when we're faced with still another problem: what wine goes with nothing?

Considering the state of the Union, the President's popularity is a little hard to understand. It kinda reminds you of the farmer talking to his neighbor. The neighbor said, "Is it true your hired hand left the gate open and half your herd wandered off?" The farmer said, "Ayah." The neighbor said, "Is that the same hired hand who broke the threshing machine, ran the tractor into the barn, and got your daughter in a family way?" The farmer said, "Ayah. Someday that fella's gonna go too far."

I hope the trainmen don't go out on strike. You don't know what it does to the economy when the only functioning railroad is Lionel.

EDUCATION

There's one thing I will never be able to understand: how a nation that has 30 million functional illiterates can still go out and earn $3 trillion a year.

A lot of schools hand out simulated diplomas at commencement and then the graduates get the real thing later on. Sometimes that applies to their education as well.

Life is a long, difficult, and expensive journey. Getting a good education is a half-fare coupon.

To err is human; to overlook it is progressive education.

I started worrying about the educational system when a kid was asked to spell "relief." He said, "R-E-L-I-E-F"—and was marked wrong.

You can't blame parents for being discouraged. I went up to an instructor and said, "Are you the new English teacher?" She said, "I are."

A lot of people are critical of modern education but at least a kid can watch a story about the Civil War on television without having his pleasure destroyed because he knows how it ends.

ELECTIONS

They say that, for the taxpayer, every election is a gamble. That's ridiculous. When you gamble there's a chance you can win.

If there's one thing I'm absolutely, definitely, positively sure of—it's the next time I'm asked my opinion, I'm Undecided.

November is the month when all Americans are preoccupied with turkeys. But enough about the elections, let's talk about Thanksgiving.

Thanksgiving is when you get to live with a turkey for weeks. Elections are when you get to live with a turkey for years.

An election is another way of getting a second opinion.

We should all be very grateful for free elections. They're our Preparation H for the seat of government.

The secrecy of the voting booth is one of America's greatest strengths. It gives all Americans the opportunity to choose our leaders, to exercise our rights, and to check our zippers.

I always get a little depressed in a voting booth. It reminds me of the living room in our new house—only larger.

The election has even affected office equipment. All over America, there are now three baskets on every desk: In, Out, and Undecided.

I didn't say the election was crooked. I just said it's the first time I ever saw an absentee ballot—from Amelia Earhart.

Poll watchers take the worry out of being close.

Elections today are so expensive, it's ridiculous. I know one candidate who's spending $800,000 and he's calling himself the underdog. Eight hundred thousand dollars and he's the underdog? How much Alpo can he eat?

Do you ever get the feeling (LOSING PARTY) candidates are picked for their ability to deliver a concession speech?

But the (LOSING PARTY) did score a few stunning upset victories. I'll bet that dogcatcher in West Lubbock thought he had that job for life!

Tolerance is (LOSING PRESIDENTIAL CANDIDATE) on January 20th humming, "I Love a Parade."

We have a transition team at our house too. It's the kids. They've taken us from rich to poor.

Then there's the couple who left the Inaugural Ball, got into their car, he sighed, turned to his wife, and said, "Does this mean we have to invite them?"

You may not jog. You may not run. You may not do knee bends. You may not do push-ups. But on November ———, at least exercise your franchise.

ELECTRIC BILLS

Abraham Lincoln read by the light of a flickering fire. I know how he felt. I've had electric bills like that myself.

Remember when you put electricity in your house because it was clean? Now you're cleaned because you put electricity in your house.

Thanks to utility companies, millions of Americans have a song on their lips. They get their electric light bill and right away they start singing: "I hate to see that evening sun go down!"

We heat our house entirely by electricity and this morning I felt impelled to call up the president of our local utility. I said, "I know people are always complaining about their electric bills but I think $75 a month is a very fair amount to pay for heating a five-room house, don't you?" He said, "I certainly do." I said, "Then why am I paying $300?"

You remember Dracula—with the two little holes that drain you dry? We have the same thing in our house. They're called electrical outlets.

ELECTRONICS

Buying an electronic game can be an emotional experience. You look at games that are so sophisticated, you begin to wonder if you're stupid. Then you look at the price tag and you no longer have to wonder.

Electronic games are the devices that bring you entertainment, challenge, information, and poverty.

Have you priced the new toys? This year there's a special name for parents who bring home electronic games—Broke-R-Us.

ENERGY CONSERVATION

Dear Mr. President: I am so upset over the way Americans waste energy, I am turning on my electric typewriter to write you this letter.

It seems to me the ultimate in recycling is a filibuster about natural gas—all that hot air over hot air.

To conserve energy, the thermostats in public buildings are being set at 78 degrees during the summer. Fortunately workers have learned to cope with it. They drink plenty of liquids; they wear light clothes; and they faint a lot.

This summer it will be very easy to identify a public building. It's where the occupants sit around singing, "Baby, it's cold outside!"

I don't have to do this for a living, you know. I could always go back to my old job, smuggling goose bumps to people in public buildings.

The building temperatures have really simplified eating for government workers. I asked one, "Do you brown-bag it or do you have a hot lunch?" He said, "Yes."

The best way to determine if your house is too cold is with a martini. If you have to chip a hole in the vermouth to get at the gin, it's too cold.

Last night we had a fireside chat at our house. We discussed who was going to go out for more wood.

My wife says she loves to stand in front of a roaring fire and hear snap, crackle, and pop. I told her to turn on the stove and eat Rice Krispies.

ENERGY SHORTAGE

Do you ever get the feeling the light at the end of the tunnel is starting to flicker again?

I'm easily confused. I can never remember if "energy crunch" is the name of a problem or a breakfast cereal.

The main thing is not to panic. Just go out and buy all the oil and gas you can—before the hoarders do.

It always bothers me when the White House claims the fuel situation is not a crisis—while down in the basement they're working on Skateboard One.

EXERCISE

I like the name of the weight-lifting team at our local seminary: the Brawn-Again Christians.

One doctor told me I ought to do some swimming. It's good for the figure. I said: "Doc, you ever see a whale?"

The trouble with these exercise programs—they're unbelievable. There's this gorgeous girl with a fantastic figure saying: "I can run the hundred yards in nine seconds flat!" That's what I mean by unbelievable. Nine seconds, maybe. Flat, never!

I love to watch those exercise programs on TV. You know the ones. Where you sit in front of the TV and they teach you how to lose all the weight you wouldn't have gained if you hadn't been sitting in front of the TV!

I call them my "garden exercises." I start off fresh as a daisy and five minutes later I'm bushed!

I don't wanna brag, but every morning I get up and my mind sends this message to my body: "Do fifty knee bends; a hundred push-ups; and run sixteen miles!" Then my body sends a message right back to my mind. It says: "Who? Me?"

The whole idea of deep breathing is you take the good air into your lungs and you push the bad air out. Now you might ask: "How do you tell the good air from the bad air?" Well, that's simple. The good air wears a white hat!

Personally, I get all the exercise I need by subscribing to forty different magazines. Every time one of them is delivered, I open it up, then I bend down to the floor to pick up the subscription card that falls out.

I bought that new book that teaches you how to make your stomach hard and flat—and it really works. You slip it in your shorts.

FARMING

The land here is so fertile, a farmer once told me it can be very dangerous, especially at planting time. Things grow so fast, you have to drop in the seed and jump back.

Farmers are really serious about using all that grain to make gasohol. Our local filling station now has three pumps—regular, premium, and whole wheat.

It isn't easy being a farmer. You spend most of your time putting things into the ground—like your savings.

If you're a farmer, you get the distinct impression that one of the food additives the government is trying to eliminate is profit.

If you want to know what the Department of Agriculture contributes to America as opposed to what our farmers contribute to America—eat a food stamp.

I worry about things like inflation or a farm strike. I mean, I'm old enough to remember eating.

FAST FOODS

GOBBLEDEGOOK: what Americans do to fast foods.

There is good news and bad news on the economic front. The good news is when you walk past a hamburger place and the sign outside reaches 50,000,000,000. The bad news is when that's the price.

Everything is relative. If you're buying a hamburger, a quarter pounder sounds great. If you're buying a bra, not so good.

I always try to encourage our local fast food restaurant in any way I can. Whenever I stop in, I go up to the owner, slap him on the back, and say, "Greasy does it!"

One fast food place even has a fortuneteller. Reads the grease on napkins.

I'll never forget the year I had Thanksgiving dinner at a fast food restaurant. It's the first time I ever said grace over grease.

America has always been able to find a use for things. Take grease. In the fifties kids put it in hair. Today we put it in fast food.

I go to one of those takeout restaurants where everything is fried. If you go there enough, what they take out is your gall bladder.

I've always had a great sympathy for Kentucky fried chicken. If I lived in Kentucky, I'd get fried too.

FATHER'S DAY

I was sleeping on the sofa when my wife and kids came in and gave me the nicest Father's Day present ever. They let me.

For Father's Day, give Dad money. It's the one thing you can be sure he doesn't have.

Even my wife honored me on Father's Day. She sent me a card addressed to THE LORD OF THE MANOR. Look how she spelled manor: M-A-N-U-R-E.

I think my wife is trying to build up my masculinity. For Father's Day she got me a Harris tweed apron.

I don't know why, but Father's Day never seems to loom as large as other holidays. It's like Mother's Day after taxes.

June (DATE) is Father's Day, when sons and daughters pay homage to dear old Dad. And as any father will tell you, it's one of the few payments that hasn't doubled in recent years.

I had good news and bad news on Father's Day. The good news is the kids all got together and sent me a check for $100 made out to CASH. The bad news is, they asked me to sign it and send it back.

My kids have no imagination, no style. They asked me what I wanted for Father's Day. I said, "You know what I've always longed for, yearned for, and dreamed about? Having breakfast in bed." So they put a cot in the kitchen.

For Father's Day my kids gave me a turtleneck sweater—and it really has an authentic turtleneck. It's green, wrinkled, and sags.

Last Father's Day my kids gave me one of those gifts that keep on giving—a lawnmower. What it keeps on giving is backaches.

Women's Lib may finally have gone too far. Now they want to know why Dad gets all the presents on Father's Day.

FLORIDA

I love Christmas in Miami Beach. Where else can you find people dreaming of a tan Christmas?

You can always tell the tourists who fly down to Florida from Canada, Maine, and Vermont and spend their entire first day on the beach. The next morning they come in two varieties—Regular and Extra Krispy.

At this time of the year, if you live in Miami and you have a guest room, there is no such thing as a distant relative.

Miami Beach hotels have come up with a great way to get Northerners to stay longer. When you get in an elevator, the Muzak plays tires spinning on ice.

There are four good reasons why I no longer have to worry about shoveling snow: I have a sixteen-year-old son, a fourteen-year-old son, a twelve-year-old son, and I live in Fort Lauderdale.

Snow is rain that couldn't afford to go to Florida.

You can always tell the New Yorkers who retire and move to Florida. When it gets too hot, they bang on the air-conditioning vent.

You can rely on one thing. No one will ever be able to make a surprise attack on Miami Beach because it has 50,000 lookouts: people who pay $225 for an ocean-front room.

Believe me, when you pay $225 for an ocean-front room, you never leave it. You just sit there staring. Each blink costs you forty-eight cents.

Have you noticed how people in Florida are always bragging about the water and the weather? For instance, the last time I went to Miami Beach, the bellboy carried four suitcases up to my room. So I gave him a quarter tip—and as he was leaving, I could hear him talking about the sun and the beach.

Last week I went down to Florida for the winter. I got it.

It's so cold in Florida, it's the first time I ever saw an orange take vitamin C.

People who go to Miami are faced with a brand-new problem this year: what do you tip the ski instructor?

You can't imagine what this weather is doing to Miami Beach. It's the first time I ever saw a pair of mittens pinned to a bikini.

Miami is very expensive at this time of year. It can cost you as much as a hundred dollars a day—and that's just for earmuffs!

FOOD

As a bachelor, I eat a lot of hamburgers. And I cook them in a way that's dear to the hearts of all bachelors. I use a microwave grease fire.

It's always interesting to argue with a health food addict. If they don't agree with you, they say you're full of bran.

People keep asking me how I always manage to be in such good spirits. I owe it all to health food. Every morning I get up and drink the juice from three martinis.

Yogurt is the magical joining together of three vital ingredients: inspired advertising, imaginative flavoring, and library paste.

Madison Avenue is the only place I know where soul food is aspirin.

I can't help but get a little depressed when I realize that Julia Child's garbage disposal eats better than I do.

You have to be impressed by modern merchandising. Now they're selling empty boxes to people who go on a fast. It's called Hunger Helper.

They were poor but they were proud. You could tell that by what they had for Sunday dinner—Gruel Wellington.

It hasn't been easy for Asians coming to live in the United States. First they have to learn how to use chopsticks to eat a typical American meal: pizza, kielbasa, and tacos.

Whoever said nothing is impossible never tried to make the Baskin-Robbins Flavor-of-the-Month Ketchup.

Every time I eat a tomato these days, I can't help but wonder if the world's proven reserve of flavor isn't declining as well.

If they really are inanimate, why do beer cans always pick the quietest part of the event to roll down the steps?

The saddest story I ever heard was about a kid who spent five years being treated for a speech impediment when all he had to do was give up peanut butter.

I still say if God had meant us to eat peanut butter He would have given us Teflon gums!

Is there anything more posh—
When indulging in a nosh,
Than eating a Hostess Twinkie—
With a sneer and an uplifted pinkie?

Now I know why they call them 100% beef hot dogs. People find out what's inside and that's what 100% of them do.

To give the kids a sense of participation, we let them make Thanksgiving dinner this year. You ever see a pizza with drumsticks?

FOOD (PRICES)

I'd say something about inflation but my mother taught me never to speak with my mouth empty.

It isn't easy being a writer, although yesterday I did write something that's worth a hundred dollars. A grocery list.

Here it is spring and it's just amazing how many Americans have green thumbs. It's from counting out twenties at the supermarket.

With today's prices, I just marvel at anyone who can call a market "super."

Be sure to be here for our next meeting because we're going to hold our annual raffle. Third prize will be an all-expenses-paid trip to Las Vegas. Second prize will be an all-expenses-paid trip to Paris. And first prize will be an all-expenses-paid trip to the supermarket.

My wife and I are going through an over-fifty crisis. Every time we get a food bill that's over fifty, there's a crisis.

One of the keys to success is to associate with people who have big money—and I do. I stand on checkout lines.

I always wanted to live life in the fast lane and I am. All I can afford at the supermarket is eight items or less.

There's a new sign at our supermarket's checkout counter. It says: ENGLISH & SPANISH SPOKEN HERE. TEARS UNDERSTOOD.

I think we're all adult enough to talk about this without embarrassment. Last Saturday night I handed a hundred-dollar bill to a girl and I'll never forget what I got in return—two bags of groceries.

What this country really needs is a chain of Richard Nixon Super-markets. When you get to the cash register, eighteen and a half inches disappear from the tape.

You can't win. We have attack dogs that protect our money and attack supermarkets that take it away.

Did you know that a warranty comes with new supermarket shopping carts? It's good for 1200 miles or $10 million, whichever it does first.

If food prices go any higher, parents won't have to teach their kids table manners. What they'll have to teach them is burping.

Thanks to food prices, the big thing today is Golf Dinners. You try to slice as little as possible.

Remember the good old days when, if you wanted a $50-a-plate dinner—you had to go out for it?

We're now in the most bountiful time of the year—when you go into a supermarket and the price of grapes is down from outrageous to exorbitant.

Grapes are $1.89 a pound. It's ridiculous. One good orgy could break you.

I don't get depressed very often but last night I suddenly realized that coffee is worth more a pound than I am.

Seafood is so high, nowadays if you find a pearl in your oyster you break even!

FOOTBALL

The (FOOTBALL TEAM) have a lot on the ball—but it's rarely hands.

Football is a game in which eleven grown men spend sixty minutes trying to move an object a hundred yards. It's a little like the post office.

Have you noticed the dance football players do in the end zone after they've scored a touchdown? It's fascinating. Either they're trying to let off steam or bring on rain!

They say football builds strong bodies, big muscles, rippling biceps. Not so. I watch it ten hours every weekend. Nothing!

Football is a great sport, but you have to admit that the people who play it are confused. Very confused. What other game has twelve gorgeous pom-pom girls standing on the sidelines and who do the players pat on the fanny? Each other!

I don't go too often but it's always exciting to see a football game live. I went to the ——————— game last Saturday and the cheerleaders were yelling: "Go, team, go, team, acupuncture, acupuncture! Go, team, go, team, acupuncture, acupuncture!" I nudged the person sitting next to me and asked, "What do they mean by acupuncture?" He said, "Stick it to them!"

They say football is too violent, which is ridiculous. Psychologists claim that professional football players are as sweet and loving and gentle as the next person—providing they're standing beside Attila the Hun.

There are certain basic things you have to learn about football. For instance, in any other sport the hipbone is connecta to the shinbone. In football, the hipbone is connecta to the stretcher.

I'm very concerned about the growing number of injuries caused by football. Last Saturday I got a shock turning on my TV set, cut my finger opening a beer can, and almost choked on a pretzel.

Have you ever seen the forward wall of the (FOOTBALL TEAM)? I have a house that doesn't have a forward wall like the (FOOTBALL TEAM)!

These fellas are so big, you only need three of them to make a dozen.

I'll tell you what the (FOOTBALL TEAM) are like. Last week, just before he took the ball, the opposing quarterback said a prayer—and a real deep voice from overhead said, "Don't get me involved!"

If you're the quarterback on the other team, you don't know whether to call a play or a cop!

My wife has developed a very explicit way of indicating she's had enough of my watching football on TV. Last Saturday she went up to the set, pointed to a player and asked, "Who's that?" I said, "That's the end." She said, "That's right," and turned it off!

The football season has ended and it's time for the annual ritual: relearning the names of your kids; replacing the springs in your couch; and you and your wife signing up for a course in Remedial Sex.

You can't really blame wives for being upset about football. It's not that they didn't know their husbands were interested in end zones. It's just that they had always assumed it was theirs.

The night after the Super Bowl, my wife put on this gorgeous gray negligee. I said, "I didn't know you had a gray negligee." She said, "I don't. It's dust."

The nice part about the football season is—nine months later obstetricians can take their vacations.

FOREIGN NATIONS

I have to give (DEBTOR NATION) credit. I didn't think anybody could need this much money and not be a relative.

I've always been fascinated by that ad for a Swiss army knife. Nowadays, what army carries knives? This is the only country I know that's protected against Limburger!

Have you noticed how few monarchies there are left in the world? For those of you who don't remember monarchies, they were mom and pop governments.

FOREIGN POLICY

I take things to heart. I really do. I still worry about Quemoy and Matsu.

The President's foreign policy hasn't been all that successful but, thinking positively, there are still many different lands we're getting along with—Maryland, Disneyland, Marineland.

The thing that intrigues me about foreign affairs is how many different people the President has to advise him. Just think of the difference this approach could have made throughout our history: "Surrender? I have not yet begun to consult!" "I regret I have but one committee to give for my country!" "Give me liberty or give me debate!" "You may kibitz when ready, Gridley!"

I liked it better when the country with "most favored nation" status was ours.

FOURTH OF JULY

In 1775 the Minutemen came into existence. That's what they were called—"Minutemen." They were great patriots but lousy lovers.

In 1776 milk and politics had a lot in common. The cream rose to the top.

We should be very grateful that Thomas Jefferson wasn't a career bureaucrat—otherwise each Fourth of July we might be celebrating the signing of the Interoffice Memo of Independence—Eyes Only.

Seventeen seventy-six is a very important date in world history. It marks one of the last revolutions that was ever fought without Cuban involvement.

The Declaration of Independence is a large stately document superbly structured, magnificently written, and beautifully produced —which carried to King George III a simple two-word message: No way!

The Fourth of July calls for something stirring, something patriotic, something really unusual—like Barbara Walters singing, "I Wuv a Pawade!"

I loved the Fourth of July speaker who got up and said, "So much has changed in the years since 1776. In 1776 the government was printing money everybody was suspicious of, but today—In 1776 inflation was getting out of hand, but today—In 1776 it took a letter seven days to go from Philadelphia to New York, but today—aw, to hell with it!"

In America, all people are created equal—although you can't help but notice that there are those who never have to go out for the coffee.

I used to love skyrockets. You'd put a match to them and things went off in all directions. These things were called "fingers."

My wife is a very protective mother. Our five-year-old was watching the Fourth of July fireworks on television. She said, "Don't stand too close!"

We only had one minor problem on July 4th. We had to ask the kids to turn down their stereo so we could hear the fireworks.

It is verified that the Liberty Bell cracked on July 8, 1835. It is probable that the warranty ran out on July 7, 1835.

FUNERALS

Lately I find myself worrying about strange things: like, when I die, should my lifetime pen be buried with me?

My uncle is an undertaker and he says it's a marvelous business. It's quiet, it's steady, it's profitable, and in twenty years he's never had a customer ask for a refund.

Funeral parlors are why the dear departed departed dear.

There's a sign downtown that has always bothered me. It says: FUNERALS—FOR ALL OCCASIONS.

Every sport has its ailment. There's tennis elbow, bowling toe and now—gambling forehead. Gambling forehead. It's when you can't decide whether to bet on 14 or 16—so you bet on 14 and 16 wins. And you go (SLAP YOUR FOREHEAD WITH THE HEEL OF YOUR HAND).

It always bothers me to put a silver dollar in a slot machine and then pull the handle down. It's the same motion you use to flush.

The other day I saw a conservationist standing in front of a casino with a big sign: DON'T SHOOT CRAPS. THEY HAVE AS MUCH RIGHT TO LIVE AS YOU DO!

GARDENING

Do you ever get the feeling that you're cutting the lawn of life with cuticle scissors?

May is a very important month for all gardeners. It's when you realize the bulbs you bought in September, planted in October, paid for in February, and expected to bloom in April—haven't.

A new house is when you have a nice green lawn and lumber to match.

For many years I thought that the grass always looked greener on the other side of the fence. Then, one day, I took off my sunglasses.

August is the month when you find yourself thinking strange thoughts, like—does Earl Scheib do lawns?

August is when you get the sneaking suspicion your lawn is using Coppertone.

> Breathes there a gardener with soul so dead
> Who to his neighbor has never said:
> "Take this zucchini, they're great cooked or raw.
> What's that? You like them? Here, take ten more!"

I was reading about that new drive-in funeral parlor and it could be a little awkward. For the first time the dear departed could get flowers and a parking ticket as well!

When I die, I want them to bury me face down. I want to see where I'm going!

There are certain things that have always bothered me. Like going into a funeral home and seeing the dear departed wearing glasses. . . . I always wonder which set they chose—the reading or the distance?

I don't know what this world is coming to. Yesterday my wife got a coupon that's good for seven cents off on a box. It was from a mortician.

It doesn't make sense—like a coffin with a lifetime guarantee.

Have you noticed how the insurance industry is trying to break new ground? Now there's an outfit that claims you *can* take it with you. It's called Mutual of Valhalla.

The best will I ever saw was this one: I, John Jones, being of sound mind, leave all my worldly possessions to my secretary, being of sound body.

Then there's the will that simply said: I, John Jones, being of sound mind—spent it!

GAMBLING

I live in a very civic-minded community. Once a week they hold a Bingo game and all the proceeds go to fight gambling.

People keep talking about legalizing gambling. I thought we already had. It's called Election Day.

America now has legalized gambling in three separate places—Las Vegas, Atlantic City, and voting booths.

I love this time of the year—when all you have to do to see the most lush, luxuriant, extravagantly colored foliage of the entire year—is turn on the TV nature programs on Sunday morning.

GAS PRICES

You think prices are high now? Wait'll you hear the latest—designer gas! You drive into a station and there are three pumps—regular, premium, and Calvin Klein.

Our friendly neighborhood gas station is now known as the Bermuda Triangle. It's where $20 bills go and are never seen again.

Motorists are now calling the platforms gas pumps are on Manhattan Islands. Every time you pull up to one—$24!

The biggest problem facing motorists today is whiplash. You get it from watching the price of gas go up.

Gas prices are now so high, they can cure you of three things—driving, idling, and hiccups.

I've had it with gas prices. This morning I got so mad, I drove down to our local filling station and told the owner to take his gas hose and shove it—right into my tank.

Last night I woke up with a start and standing at the foot of my bed was a very old man with a gallon of thirty-nine-cent gasoline. It was the Ghost of Christmas Past.

I'm very disappointed in my rich uncle who died last week. He left the Rolls to me and the gas to my sister.

And now, a special message to filling stations all over America: jack up the car, not the gas!

Now I know why they're called service stations. You know what you get when you're being serviced.

GAS SHORTAGE

Frankly, I'd be more worried about the future if our gas tanks were full and our think tanks were empty.

The gas shortage is altering our values. This morning someone told me there's a filling station in Burbank that has naked starlets pumping gas. I said, "No-lead or regular?"

I have only one question for people who live their lives in the fast lane: where do you get the gas?

Gas rationing would guarantee every American getting enough. If that's so, forget gas—ration sex!

They say that even garbage can be made into gasoline. Why not? It's already being made into movies, books, and TV shows.

GAS STATIONS

Remember the good old days when opportunity knocked and car engines didn't? . . . I brought my brand-new car back to the dealer. I said, "Every time I go up a hill it sounds like castanets. What should I do?" And he was very helpful. He said, "Hum 'Malaguena.' "

The dealer said, "It's the no-lead gas. It doesn't have enough octane to do the job." I said, "Please. I get enough of that from my wife."

It used to be that you paid $8000 for a car and the engine purred like a kitten. Mine sounds like it's clearing its throat.

Gas stations are now divided into two separate sections. One section is where everything is done for you. That's called "Full Service." The other section is where nothing is done for you. That's called "Civil Service."

Where else but in America can you see people who make $50,000 a year pumping their own gas, while a kid gets paid $3.35 an hour to sit on a stool and watch them?

This morning I drove into a filling station and it was very discouraging. The fella pumping gas didn't check the oil, didn't clean the windshield, let the gas overflow, and then lost the gas cap. What made it so discouraging, it was self-service.

You know what I hate about self-service? It's always so bad.

GIFTS

I hate packages that are so beautifully wrapped up, what's inside is a disappointment. I got enough of that on my honeymoon.

I try to give useful gifts. For instance, if I know someone has been sent a set of fine china by parcel post, I'll give something that will come in handy when they open it—smelling salts.

I don't want you to get the impression my in-laws don't bring things. They do, but it's always a problem. How do you gift-wrap an appetite?

I bought a $10,000 5-karat white diamond through the mail. It's called a white diamond because, when you find out what it's worth, that's what you turn.

It's the sort of a gift you pull out of the box while looking for the present.

GOD

Some people only turn to God when they need something. It's like praying collect.

Spring is God looking down at this battered old world and saying: "One more time!"

Maybe we'd better stop complaining so much about what's wrong with this world. God might want to take it back to the shop.

I hate to be interrupted while praying. There's something about putting God on hold.

It's nice to know that Henry Kissinger hasn't lost any of his old self-confidence. Yesterday someone said, "God help us!"—and Henry said, "I'll try."

God is not dead. He's just getting a second opinion.

God is not dead. He just moved a little farther back.

GOLD

All that glitters is gold.

The gold scene is like this. My wife went into a jewelry store to buy an 18-karat necklace. The owner brought one out, she tried it on, studied it in a mirror, and said, "It's nice, but I'd really like one that's a little more expensive." He said, "No problem. Come back tomorrow."

With gold at $——— an ounce, people are thinking of their fillings as an asset. That's right. I was at a roulette table in Vegas and I saw three things bet on red—a $5.00 chip, a $10 chip, and a head.

The first thing I do each morning is get the paper, turn to the financial section, and look up the price of gold. It's such a good feeling to know that, overnight, your mouth has gone up $42.

I love the way they always refer to the price of gold "at the afternoon fixing." I don't know who's fixing it but I think it's my auto mechanic.

Now I know why retirement is called "the golden years." Every day the price goes up a little more.

GOLF

Sunday is the day when we bow our heads. Some of us are praying and some of us are putting.

I love to watch other people out at the golf course. For instance, you can always spot an employee playing golf with his boss. He's the one who gets a hole in one and says, "Ooops!"

Putting is the most difficult part of playing golf. It calls for intense concentration, perfect timing, and a surefire grip. It's a little like dating.

Concentration is when you can complete your putt between your caddy's ah-ah-ah-ah and choooooo!

Golf is a marvelous sport. Where else could you spend the afternoon with three hookers—score—and your wife doesn't get mad?

A golfer went out to Los Angeles International Airport and asked the price of a ticket to New York. The clerk said, "Four hundred dollars." He said, "Good. Give me a ticket to Miami." The clerk said, "I thought you wanted to go to New York." The golfer said, "I do—but you don't know my hook!"

Playing golf is a little like carving a turkey. It helps if you have your slice under control.

A straight line is the shortest distance between two points. Now if we could only convince golfers.

The weather forecast is six inches of snow mixed with sleet and freezing rain, plus sixty-mile-an-hour winds. Well—maybe I'll play just nine holes today.

January is when golfers rely on three basic clubs: a Jack Nicklaus driver, an Arnold Palmer putter, and a Sears Roebuck shovel.

Have you ever played golf during a hurricane? It's the first time I ever got a hole in none.

I go to a very patriotic golf course. Every time I call them up to reserve a starting time, their answer is: "Oh, say, can you tee by the dawn's early light?"

Golf is getting so expensive. I won't say what they charge for carts but you get the distinct impression that all of the shafts aren't on putters.

I was totaling up what I've paid our local golf club for membership dues, special assessments, rentals, lessons, restaurant tabs, bar bills, and tips. Maybe they ought to call the next tournament the Wallet Open.

The best way to improve your golf game is to think of them as express holes—for four strokes or less.

> Different strokes for different folks,
> It's there for all to see:
> 68 for Arnold Palmer—
> 99, alas, for me.

You have to be a little suspicious of anyone who writes down his golf score and then wipes his fingerprints off the pencil.

We have a lot to learn from golf. Remember the sinking of the *Titanic?* It never would have happened if that iceberg had yelled: "Fore!"

As a weekend golfer, I have one all-consuming ambition in life—to live to be a hundred. I always wanted to shoot my age.

They call the MX a movable missile. The way I play, so is my golf ball.

> Oh, bury me not on the eighteenth tee;
> Where the golf pros howl—and I think at me.

I've had very bad luck with golf. Very bad luck. One time a minister suggested that before every swing I bow my head, close my eyes, and pray. So I bowed my head, closed my eyes, and prayed— and somebody stole my clubs.

I didn't realize how preoccupied I had become with golf until I went to church, the minister said, "Let us pray," I clasped my hands and it was an interlocking grip.

Let me live in a house by the side of a golf course and be a friend to doctors.

Behavioral scientists once spent three years teaching a gorilla to hit a golf ball. And they were so proud of this accomplishment, they held a press conference at a well-known country club. Then, as the reporters took notes and the television cameras recorded it for posterity, the gorilla swung and hit the ball a magnificent 280 yards to within three feet of the cup. Tumultuous applause. Then they move to the green in breathless anticipation of history being made. The gorilla lines up the shot, pulls the club back—and hits the ball another 280 yards.

GOVERNMENT

Have you ever considered how much a State of the Union address is like a 28-inch snowfall? It's deep, it covers everything, it affects us all—and six months later you'd never know it happened.

The Administration is really moving along. Someone just saw a report entitled "The Study to Eliminate Redundancy Study."

You can count on one thing with federal regulations: the mumbo is always jumbo.

The President is determined to reorganize the government. He even has a name for it: The Interstate Myway System.

I asked an old-timer in Washington what effect the President's reorganization plan would have on the federal bureaucracy. He said, "Fill a pail with water." I did. He said, "Now stick your hand in the water as far as it will go." I did. He said, "Now pull it out." I did. He said, "Now look for the hole."

To err is human. To shrug is civil service.

Civil service is the system that government employees work under —and occasionally provide.

Government regulators are a lot like brand-new Boy Scouts—they help you across the street even if you don't want to go.

Government regulation is like ketchup. You either get too little or too much.

The only thing business has to fear is FEAR itself: Federal Enforcement of Archaic Regulations.

I don't know about decontrol. It sure hasn't worked with our kids.

Washington had better be careful. If taxes and inflation get any worse, pretty soon there won't be enough poverty to go around.

If you stop to think about it, big government isn't really too different from big business. Big government has a chief executive—the President. It has a board of directors—the Congress. It has a corporate headquarters—Washington, D.C. It has a purchasing department—the G.S.A. It has a security force—the army, navy, coast guard, and air force. And it even has a complaint department—Jack Anderson.

The best training for government is to be a member of your college rowing team. You're already used to looking one way and going another.

I'm for cutting military spending but that latest proposal may be going too far—coin-operated guns.

There's an association for virtually every interest. A new group is called Relatives in Public Office—RIP-OFF for short.

GRADUATION

A graduation ceremony is where the commencement speaker tells 2000 students dressed in identical caps and gowns that individuality is the key to success.

Nowadays, if you tell graduates the future is theirs—they don't know if it's a promise or a threat.

A graduation ceremony is where the speaker says: "The future is in your hands"—and it's the same kids who throw your newspaper into the bushes.

I was sitting next to a teacher who said she always enjoys going to graduation ceremonies because she sees the same symbolism as in Western movies. I said, "How do graduation ceremonies have the same symbolism as Western movies?" She said, "The villains are wearing black hats."

Graduation exercises are very important. It's one of the few times schools pay attention to passers who aren't on the football team.

Actually, wearing those heavy black graduation gowns on a hot June afternoon is ideal preparation for the real world. It gets them used to sweating.

I won't say what the future holds for June graduates, but there's a lesson to be learned from their graduation gowns—no pockets.

It's interesting how quickly kids adapt to reality. I just saw a June graduate in a department store buying a necktie. He asked if it came with instructions.

This is a very traumatic time of the year for students. On graduation day they're told the future is in their hands. Then they go out and look for a job and learn that the present isn't.

Everything is relative. To a June graduate, B.A. stands for Bachelor of Arts. To a July employer, it stands for Barely Able.

Commencement is when the real world beckons to the graduate—but not always with the right finger.

HALLOWEEN

I love Halloween. It's the only night of the year rock stars look natural.

California is where they go in for very unusual Halloween parties. For instance, this year they're going to fill a big tub with real estate ads—and bob for mortgages.

I went to a Halloween party for middle-class taxpayers who have three kids in college. We filled a big tub with debts and bobbed for loans.

I've been on a 900-calorie-a-day diet for the last two months and I can't help it: I know just how I'm going to celebrate Halloween. I'm going to fill a vat with spaghetti and bob for meatballs!

It's all right to scare people, but this year I think kids are over-doing it. I saw one of them dressed up as a heating oil bill.

Last Halloween there was a knock on the door, I opened it and there were my three kids dressed up as the scariest thing I could ever imagine—my three kids!

Halloween is when kids put on strange outfits to startle adults. In our house—that would be a suit.

For a real old-fashioned Halloween, let's all go down and tip over Cuba.

HEALTH

And so, as we wend our way through the peaks and Valiums of life . . .

The next time you feel like complaining about your health—think of all the lifetime guarantees you've outlived.

Tense is when you have to take Maalox to settle the bicarbonate.

As a kid I had a calcium deficiency. A real calcium deficiency. I once broke a tooth on grits.

Words seem to have lost all meaning. Yesterday I went into a medical supply house to get a wheelchair. The clerk said, "Use it in good health!"

It's only a question of time before we have a government health insurance program. It's either that or nationalize Lourdes.

Heart attacks are the high cost of livid.

Tranquilizers are what allow you to walk through the storm with your head held—high.

A placebo is when you practice medicine without a medicine.

HECKLERS

Sir, may I suggest you're having all the impact of a 10¢ OFF coupon on the federal budget?

You have some wonderful thoughts but they haven't quite worked their way through to your mouth.

You're a little confused. This is a lecture. Your mind should be open, not your mouth.

I have a great idea. Let's play "Library." You be the silence.

If there's such a thing as reincarnation, you're going to come back as a wet blanket.

Have you ever heard of human rights? You are human, right?

Having listened to your humble opinion—and I must say it has every right to be . . .

Have you ever considered living a life of *quiet* desperation?

I feel it only fair to warn you that what you have just said is the oral equivalent of war.

That's a very profound thought—although I know very few pros who would want to be found with it.

HOLIDAYS

February is the month in which we celebrate the birthdays of our two greatest Presidents: George Washington, who was the father of our country—and Abraham Lincoln, who was the marriage counselor.

I always find Lincoln Day sales confusing. You're never quite sure if you're honoring the man for freeing the slaves in the South or the inventory in the stores.

Abraham Lincoln was born in a one-room log cabin in Kentucky. Today, Lincoln is hailed as one of our great Presidents. Kentucky is hailed as one of our great states. And that one-room log cabin is hailed as a steal at $94,000.

I went out to buy a box of Valentine candy and learned a great truth: it's a lot cheaper to have lust in your heart than chocolates.

St. Patrick's Day is when things must be green to be appreciated.

For the Irish, St. Patrick's Day is a real success story. They drive to pubs in a $10,000 car and leave in a $40,000 paddy wagon.

The Labor Day weekend is when you hear the cry of the open road. It's saying: "Stay home! Stay home!"

I had a rather busy Labor Day holiday weekend. First I had to explain what a holiday is to my wife. Then I had to explain what labor is to our kids.

Do you realize there are three million Indians in this country who wish Columbus had been on Standby?

You can't blame Indians for being upset. To the world, Columbus was a great explorer. To the Indians, he was a subdivider.

HOMEOWNERS

A homeowner is someone who will pick up the Sunday newspaper, see a headline saying: END OF THE WORLD IMMINENT!—and read the Sears ad first.

In the spring I mow the lawn. In the summer I clean the pool. In the fall I rake the leaves. In the winter I shovel the snow. Lincoln didn't really free the slaves. He just let homeowners take their place.

You have to admire the American spirit. Where else but in America can somebody borrow the $10,000 down payment from a relative, get a $60,000 first mortgage, a $30,000 second mortgage—and be called a homeowner?

My wife is one of those people who really knows what she wants. I mean, if heaven doesn't have washers and dryers, she ain't going.

HOMES (DECORATION)

We just bought a new kitchen range and the price was unbelievable. It's the first time an oven ever cleaned *us!*

We just bought a microwave oven and it's really great. It's the first time I ever got police calls on a roast beef.

My wife forgot that this year she has a microwave oven. You ever eat Thanksgiving dinner at seven in the morning?

My wife is redecorating the house again. We've had this house eighteen years now. I won't say how many times she's redecorated, but she's never had to dust!

And she's always getting rid of furniture 'cause it clashes with something else—like our savings! . . . My wife is so hipped on color harmony, she's done a very unusual thing. She's decorated an entire fourteen-room house around the color of one object. Our Princess telephone. What makes it so unusual, it's black! . . . No matter what time it is anywhere in the world—in our home it's midnight!

I bought one of those big round beds and it's driving me out of my mind. How do you make hospital corners?

HOMES (MORTGAGES)

Today I did what I have been dreaming of doing all of my life—I bought a $300,000 house. Well, it isn't exactly a $300,000 house. It's a $60,000 house with a 13% mortgage.

Remember when the biggest problem was paying off the mortgage instead of getting one?

Our values are changing. I saw a tombstone with the inscription: HOLDER OF THE MEDAL OF HONOR, THE LEGION OF MERIT, AND A 5% MORTGAGE.

Remember when people burned mortgages instead of vice versa?

We've now reached the Seven Dwarfs stage of taking out a mortgage. When you go into the bank, you're Bashful. When you hear that mortgages are still available, you're Happy. When you're told the rate, you're Grumpy. And if you accept it, you're Dopey.

You can always tell the bitter homeowners. They have a sign in their front yard: BEWARE OF MORTGAGE.

Our neighbors have had to give up their car, movies, bowling, picnics, travel, and vacations to meet their mortgage payments— but at least it has helped the youngest kid with his school lessons. Last night he looked up from his history book and asked, "What's a debtor's prison?" And his mother said, "Look around, son. Just look around."

Nowadays everything in a house is built in. The cabinets are built in; the washing machine is built in; the dryer is built in; and, thanks to the mortgage rate, there's even something else that's built in—poverty!

The newest trend in houses is six rooms and no baths. The mortgage keeps you cleaned.

Lincoln freed the slaves. Now if we could only convince the holders of thirty-year, 16% mortgages . . .

HOMES (PRICES)

The first thing you learn when you go out looking is that the term "fair housing" has nothing to do with the price.

When a builder advertises a new house as a "steal," I wish they'd define who is the stealer and who is the stealee.

Now I know why they say your home is your castle. It looks like a home but it costs like a castle.

> I went to look at new houses
> But the prices were mighty strange.
> One hundred to two hundred thousand—
> I'll never be home in that range.

I wish they wouldn't refer to things "in the $100,000 range." You're never quite sure if they're referring to the house of today or the oven of 1990.

When you pay $100,000 for a house that's worth $35,000—with a 13% mortgage and $2000-a-year heating bills—you finally know why we no longer call the principal space "the living room." This is living?

I won't say how expensive buying a new home is, but if the Welcome Wagon really wants to do something worthwhile—forget the coupons, samples, and maps—bring a payment!

They interviewed that fella who won the million-dollar lottery and asked him what he was going to do with the money. He said, "Well, first, I'm going to buy me a tract house. And if there's anything left . . ."

We went out with a real estate broker to look at houses and it's interesting how many people now have names for their houses. We looked at one place for $185,000 and the name over the door was Stately Manor. We looked at another place for $135,000 and the name over the door was Rolling Meadow. And you might find this hard to believe, but we looked at a house for $18,000 and even that had a name over the door—Fido.

There was an old lady who lived in a shoe. It was all she could find for $80,000.

The big thing today is garage sales. That's when you spend $90,000 for a house that's the size of a garage.

You can always tell an American by the house he buys. He'll scrimp and save and budget and cut corners—and when he finally can afford a $30,000 house, he'll buy one—for $60,000!

It's amazing how small the new houses are. We looked at one that advertised a cathedral ceiling in the living room. I said, "Cathedral ceiling! It's eight feet high." The broker said, "That's right." I said, "Then why do you call it a cathedral ceiling?" He said, "You take one look at it and say, 'Good God!' "

There's one thing about buying a new house I'll never understand. You spend three weeks shopping for an $800 used car for your daughter. But you spend ten minutes looking at a $190,000 house. Then you say to your wife, "Let's take it. We'll be late for the movies!"

And the questions they ask you when you buy a house. The salesman said, "I assume you have money in the bank." I said, "Of course I have money in the bank." He said, "How much?" I said, "I dunno. Let me shake it!"

I love the way new houses feature an eat-in kitchen. By the time you finish paying for it, you don't have enough money to eat out!

I don't wanna start any trouble, but I don't believe all those stories about how poor Abraham Lincoln was. Do you know how much a house with a fireplace costs?

Nowadays the first thing you learn when you go to buy firewood is —it's cheaper to burn money.

We're living in unusual times. You spend ten minutes sitting on the leather chairs of the builder when you buy your house. You spend twenty minutes sitting on the leather chairs of the lawyer when you close on your house. And then you spend thirty years sitting on the orange crates in your living room while you pay for your house.

HOMES (REPAIRS)

Have you looked at new houses lately? I can remember when, if you took a thirty-year mortgage, you wondered if you'd last that long. Now you wonder if the house will last that long.

I don't want to complain about our builder, but you've heard the expression "halfway house"? We bought one.

I know all about cluster bombs. I once bought a town house.

I'll never forget the first house we ever bought. There were three things green about it—the shutters, the lumber, and us.

It's only after you've moved into the house that you start to question little things. Like, why was the architect always wearing a ski mask?

I love that title "The Invisible Man." It's what happens to your builder two minutes after the closing.

The builder says there's nothing wrong with the weather stripping in our house. So how come we have the only vacuum cleaner on the block with snow tires?

I don't want to complain about the workmanship in our new house, but yesterday Opportunity knocked on our door—and did $135 worth of damage.

If you've never dealt with a contractor, there are some things you should know. For instance, they are not deformed. It's just that, after you've bought the house, they get that way from shrugging.

The first thing you learn when you buy a new house is, you don't live in the house. You sleep in the house. You live in the hardware store.

A hardware store is a fascinating place. Where else can you spend $125 to buy all those things you need to fix all those things that don't need fixing?

Try to get help in this weather. Last night at midnight I called up a furnace repairman. I said, "The furnace conked out and I'm freezing to death." He said, "Read two *Playboys* and call me in the morning."

Sometimes you learn that your pipes have frozen in a very dramatic way—like turning on your washing machine and watching your shorts hit an iceberg.

I really don't know about these things. One time a plumber said he was going to bring his plumber's helper. I set out drinks for the three of us!

A house can be a pleasure if you have a home handyman's book. Then, whenever something goes wrong, you get out the book, find a handyman who's home, and call him!

But after a while you get used to it. We've had so many repairmen in our house, every bathroom has three towels: HIS, HERS, and GREASY!

Things are always going wrong with a house. Yesterday my wife called the plumber and when he came in he said, "Where's the drip?" She said, "Upstairs trying to fix the leak!"

I won't say what our basement looks like but last week it won a Venice Look-Alike Contest.

I love the terminology they use with houses—like a "finished basement." When, in the history of home building, has anyone ever been finished with a basement? We have so many leaks, if Moses were alive today, he wouldn't part the Red Sea. What he'd part is our basement!

It got so bad, one day I called up the contractor and said, "We have termites in our basement." He said, "What are they doing?" I said, "The backstroke!"

You know what really upset me about our house? When I heard a termite refer to it as junk food!

The salesman said, "There's a thousand little extras about this house you don't notice at first." He was right. They're called termites.

Frankly, I've become very paranoid about my house. I still think what the aluminum is siding against is me!

HOSPITAL COSTS

I'm just fascinated by modern medicine. Nowadays the very same operation can add ten years to your life and take ten years off your savings.

Everything is so expensive. What hospitals really need is cheaper equipment—like an X-ray machine that takes four poses for a quarter.

Our local hospital is trying to keep down costs and it's really necessary. I mean, I don't mind legitimate hospital expenses, but I think a coin-operated bedpan is going too far.

The bills you get from a hospital are always interesting. Most of the time they're in the form of a computer printout. A computer, I might add, that got its training at a used car lot.

Everything on a hospital bill is itemized. You look up at your I.V. and you know that bottle is costing you $9.75. I always figure for $9.75 the least they could do is dress it up a little. Add a touch of garlic, a sprig of parsley, an olive.

But I happen to know that hospitals are trying to conserve. If you don't believe it, look at the hospital gowns they give you to wear.

In the area of conservation, one of the things hospitals are doing is recycling the food. Didn't you know that? Let's face it, when have you ever met anybody who ever ate a hospital meal? I had a hamburger that was so old, you didn't season it—you dusted it!

HOSPITALS

Municipal hospitals are where you can't understand the doctors because they're Asian, African, and European. Private hospitals are where you can't understand the doctors because they're doctors.

A lot of towns have signs saying: SLOW—HOSPITAL. I think they were put up by people who rang for the nurse.

What ever happened to good old-fashioned medicine? I can remember when the first thing that happened when you were rushed to a hospital was, they took your pulse. Now what they take is your Blue Cross number.

For those of you who have never seen a hospital gown, it's sort of an intensive bare unit.

I don't know of anyone who feels comfortable in a hospital gown. How could you? The front is rated G and the back is rated X. . . . Now I know what they mean by southern exposure.

The real agony of hospitals is, everybody is running around half naked and you're too sick to look. . . . That's right. That's how they tell if you're getting well. The first time you do a double take —out!

I try to go to one of those friendly hospitals. The kind that offer three back rubs a day. One you get. Two you give.

If you're a fella, there's always a lot of fantasy attached to things that happen in hospitals—like back rubs. Have you ever had a back rub in a hospital? It's like being invited to a liquor cabinet for Kool-Aid. . . . A hospital back rub is like a massage parlor run by Women's Lib.

HOTELS

It's great the way hotels worry about you. For instance, they always put drinking glasses in little paper bags marked: THIS GLASS HAS BEEN SANITIZED FOR YOUR PROTECTION. And they really are. The glass has been sanitized. The lipstick on the rim has been sanitized. The crack down the side has been sanitized.

I don't know what goes on upstairs but have you looked at the Bible in your room? It only has Seven Commandments.

Thanks to inflation, you check into a hotel and right away you run into the Sawbuck Problem. You give the bellhop a buck and does he get sore!

Have you been to the hotel restaurant yet? I won't say what they charge for a chicken dinner but it's the last time I'm gonna pay an arm and a leg for a wing and a breast!

I would also like to pay tribute to the hotel coffee shop and their religious prices: $4.25 for a hamburger, $1.75 for a piece of pie, and $1.50 for a cup of coffee. I say religious prices because they remind me of a quotation from the Bible: "I was a stranger and ye took me in."

INCOME TAX

What can you really say about the income tax? It's the ketchup on the Beef Wellington of life.

January to April is always a very exciting time of the year. It's when we go from the Super Bowl to the Super Bill.

April is when millions of taxpayers have a long form and a short fuse.

April is the month of the 1040—or 680 Celsius.

Dry cleaners will tell you the greatest spot remover ever invented is the 1040. It removes five-spots, ten-spots . . .

Nothing makes filling out a 1040 easier than having enough proof —86 proof.

Today is the tomorrow you worried about yesterday. If today is April 15th, you were right!

It's income tax time again and this year I'm going to be prepared for it. I just enrolled in the Evelyn Wood School of Speed Paying.

Sometimes I wish I were a scholar. I've always wanted to read the instructions for the income tax in the original Greek.

The income tax code is unique. It's the only code that breaks you.

The first few lines of the 1040 ask for your name, address, and Social Security number. You can either consider this vital statistics or foreplay.

Have you seen the new tax forms this year? They're much more realistic. Where your wife signs, it says ACCOMPLICE.

They've lowered the instructions for the income tax from a twelfth-grade reading level to an eighth-grade level. If that doesn't work, there are contingency plans to lower it to a fifth-grade level. And if that doesn't work, they have one last desperate plan. They'll put the whole thing on H & R Blocks.

The instructions for the income tax have been written on an eighth-grade level. You can tell that from the first paragraph: YOU, TARZAN. ME, I.R.S.

The I.R.S. had no choice but to simplify the instructions. I understand that last year 32% of the questions were answered, "Huh?"

Everything is designed for the eighth-grade mentality. For instance, the tax booklet now comes with two returns. One you fill out and the other you color.

And the eighth-grade concept is followed all the way through. For instance, if you don't finish everything on your tax table, you don't get dessert.

Sitting down at the dining-room table to fill out your tax return is a bit of Americana—sort of a Norman Rockwell picture with a Norman Mailer vocabulary.

You can always tell when people are working on their income tax. In a very calm, orderly manner they clean off the dining-room table, make neat stacks of all their canceled checks and receipts, sharpen a half-dozen pencils, open the booklet of instructions, and set to work. Then an hour later they stand up, stretch their arms, and kick the cat.

At income tax time, T.G.I.F. stands for only one thing: Thank God It's Finished!

Vacation time is when you get away from it all. Income tax time is when they get it all away from you.

Watching an accountant fill out your income tax returns is always a fascinating experience. It's like putting your savings on hold.

I have my taxes done by a very considerate, a very compassionate fella. He's the only accountant I know with a recovery room.

I'm against having other people do your tax returns. I don't think we should make confusion a spectator sport.

It's just amazing some of the deductions people take. One businessman tried to deduct $800 for massage parlors. Listed it under "Hired Hands."

> When it comes to paying your taxes,
> And it's more than you thought it would cost,
> Keep in mind that wise old saying:
> That he who hesitates is forced.

You can always tell the procrastinators on April 15th. They're the ones who mail the 1040 at 10:40.

I just paid my income tax. I wonder if Lourdes works on checkbooks.

Around April 15th, do you ever get the feeling that someone has flushed your wallet?

You know what's great about this country? The sheer equality of it. Where else but in America do you have sharecroppers and millionaires—and they both wind up paying the same taxes!

INDIANS

In 1621 the Indians had the same problem with land that we have with money. They never had so much or saw it go so fast.

Indians were invited to the first Thanksgiving dinner and they had a marvelous time right up until the entertainment—when three Pilgrims started singing: "This land is your land, this land is my land."

I just can't get over how ungrateful the American Indians are. Three centuries ago our forefathers invited them to an outdoor Thanksgiving dinner. Now they want to take back the restaurant.

I just can't understand how primitive peoples ever managed. For instance, have you ever tried to wash things by slamming them against a flat rock? It's tough enough on clothes but on dishes it's murder!

INFLATION

Inflation is when you're wealthy and you no longer can afford the things you bought when you were poor.

Government economists say the increase in the rate of inflation is temporary. Consumers know it's a long way from temporary.

Remember when what you now pay for a TV set could buy you a car? What you now pay for a car could buy you a town house? And what you now pay for a town house could buy you a town?

Even the old proverbs don't make sense anymore. Nowadays a penny saved is ridiculous.

America never did produce a good five-cent cigar, but it's working on a good five-cent dollar.

We're living in troubled times. Last week a fella petitioned to have his name legally changed to Inflation—because he loves to get whipped.

Kinky sex is when you love something that's inflatable—like the dollar.

Inflation is when everybody who retired on a fixed income is in the same boat—the *Titanic*.

Maybe it's time we all read that bumper sticker about the economy. The one that says: I BRAKE FOR INFLATION.

I have the same reaction to inflation that I have to Howard Cosell: will it never stop?

RAISE HELL, NOT PRICES!

GET RID OF INFLATION FOREVER—MAIL IT!

What America really needs is better craftsmanship. Look at inflation. Every time we get a handle on it, it comes off.

Dear Secretary of the Treasury: I'm writing this penny postcard that I bought for thirteen cents, to tell you people what a wonderful job you're doing in controlling inflation.

Is it true that elevators at the Department of Commerce now have two buttons? One is marked DOWN and the other is marked COST OF LIVING?

Basically, the Administration is taking a basketball approach to inflation. They want to dribble credit and slam-dunk prices.

Incidentally, in this technological age, we no longer refer to it as "inflation." It's a nest-egg meltdown.

There is only one sure way to slow down inflation. Turn it over to the post office.

INSECTS

I blame cockroaches on Noah. I really do. When he had the two of them in the ark, why didn't he just go (STAMP ON FLOOR)?

There is so much injustice in the world! I just read that cockroaches are now four hundred million years old—and not once has anyone ever sung, "Happy Birthday to You!"

But even mosquitoes have problems. Two of them landed on Dolly Parton. Twenty minutes later one turned to the other and said, "I don't know about you, but I'm full!"

INSULTS

I know you have a great respect for precise thinking—and that's why you're using it so sparingly.

Sir, how does it feel to be a tap dancer in the canoe of life?

I didn't say he was clumsy, I just said if he ever took up Transcendental Meditation his mantra would be Ooops!

I can't understand why people call him a malingerer. It's the best thing he does.

WHEN SOMEBODY SPILLS SOMETHING: If you don't mind, I'd like to call you by your generic name—a klutz.

Sir, is your name Hollandaise? I notice you're always on the sauce.

If this man had greatness thrust upon him, he'd ask if it comes with instructions.

Dumb? He'd need a cue card just to say, "Huh?"

If they ever run an ad for a klutz, don't apply. You're overqualified.

INTEREST RATES

It's very discouraging to see what deficit spending has done to interest rates. The more we prime the pump, the more it pumps the prime.

We are truly living in an economic democracy. You can go into any bank in the country, take out a loan, and get the same interest rate you could formerly only get from Big-Nose Louie.

I'm a sensualist. I love to run my fingers over the expensive things in life—silks, satins, furs, and loans.

A bank is an institution that is always concerned with the best interest of its community. Lately, the best interest has been 13%.

Interest rates are now so high, it's a heartrending sight to go to Beverly Hills and see people standing in line for mortgage stamps.

INTERNAL REVENUE SERVICE

April is when the I.R.S. really does a number on us—1040.

There's a reason why the income tax regulations are so lengthy and detailed. Anyone worth doing is worth doing well!

April 15th is when we realize there are no atheists in I.R.S. waiting rooms. Let us bow our heads and pay.

The Internal Revenue Service is the nearest thing we have to a Chinese dinner. No matter how much you give them, a year later they're hungry again.

Here it is April—the month when I.R.S. holds its annual B.Y.O.B. party. Bring Your Own Bundle.

Have you noticed that, whenever you get your act together, the I.R.S. is the ticket taker?

Have you seen the latest? A see-through barrel. It's from Frederick's of I.R.S.

Doctors say that if you overtax your body it just collapses. Don't tell us. Tell the I.R.S.

A taxpayer called up the I.R.S. to ask if he could take a certain deduction on his income tax. The answer was "No!"—followed by "This is a recorded announcement."

This is the time of year when you hear weird conversations, like:
"I just got back from the cleaners."
"I thought you went to the I.R.S."
"That's right."

Redundancy is the I.R.S. asking Dolly Parton to fill out her form.

You can't blame the I.R.S. for being worried. How would you feel if you had a $100 billion owed to you—and it was all coming by mail?

Did you ever feel like telling the I.R.S., "Not this year. I have a headache."

The I.R.S. may call it the Estimated Income Tax. I call it foreplay.

INTRODUCTIONS

It is a very special pleasure to introduce our dinner speaker. We may have a butter substitute. We may have a sugar substitute. And we may have a cream substitute—but tonight our speaker is the real thing.

Our next speaker is a man who has risen to every occasion. His colleagues are impressed; his competitors are amazed; and his wife is delighted.

WHEN INTRODUCING THE GUEST OF HONOR AT A ROAST: And now, presenting the case for the defense, ——————!

Those speeches really hit the spot. And now, I have a feeling the spot is going to hit back.

I've known our guest of honor as a man, as an adolescent, and as a child—sometimes on the same day.

I must admit the Program Committee had a difficult decision to make concerning this evening. They didn't know whether to announce our guest of honor and charge $25 to get in—or, after you were in, to announce our guest of honor and charge $50 to get out.

Our guest tonight spoke to us last year and did turn-away business. Over a hundred people saw his name on the program and turned away.

Our next speaker is a man of many accomplishments—the inventor of the copper trapeze for arthritic aerialists.

This speech was made possible by a grant from the Treasurer and a grunt from the Program Chairman.

INTRODUCTIONS

(RESPONDING TO)

Wasn't that a lovely introduction? He must write the words for tombstones!

I wish you hadn't called me a self-made man. Up till now I've been trying to share the blame.

AFTER A GLOWING INTRODUCTION: On a hot summer's night like this, I can't tell you how good it feels to get a snow job like that.

First, let me thank you for that marvelous introduction. If I were standing any taller, my ears would pop.

I dunno. Whenever I hear an introduction like that, I'm always tempted to respond with a four-letter word—TRUE!

Whenever I get a big buildup like that I make it a practice never to tell an audience I don't deserve it. I figure they're going to find that out soon enough.

I'm not one to blow my own horn so it's always nice to have a Gabriel introduce you.

First, I'd like to ask for a copy of that introduction. Then, the next time anyone ever says to me, "Who do you think you are?"—am I gonna have an answer!

It's just wonderful hearing an introduction like that. It's like a verbal tombstone.

AFTER A NEEDLING INTRODUCTION: The acoustics in here are really terrible. I heard every word he said.

I think I'm the victim of a hit-and-run emcee.

This has really been a memorable evening. It's the first time I ever went to a funeral where I was the corpse.

An introduction like that always reminds me of baking an apple pie in a microwave oven. It's short, it's sweet, but it still has a lot of crust!

After an introduction like that, anything I do now is a comeback.

Something tells me I've just had a vasectomy done on my reputation.

It's always a pleasure to be introduced by —————, particularly in the summertime. His talent, like his suit, is always so light-weight.

I'll say one thing for —————: when he comes on, the program really picks up speed. That's what happens when you go downhill.

That was —————, the Three Mile Island of comedy.

AFTER A VERY LONG INTRODUCTION: Do you realize, if I were one of those speakers who needs no introduction, we would have been home by now?

INVENTIONS

This announcement may be a bit premature, but I happen to be working on an invention that will free us forever from our dependence on foreign heating oil. It's a windup furnace!

Society only rewards success. What about some of the great inventions that didn't work—like chastity suspenders?

I happen to be the inventor of the solar pacemaker. There's only one problem. When the sun goes out, so do you.

Have you noticed how businessmen are never accorded the full honors they deserve? Americans honor Alexander Graham Bell, the inventor of the telephone. But not one person will ever honor Mordecai Genghis Snerd, the inventor of the telephone bill!

A research organization analyzed 5000 typical phone conversations and came to the reluctant conclusion that the telephone was invented by Alexander Graham Bull.

The invention of the telephone would probably have made a fantastic contribution to our ability to communicate if it hadn't been for one previous event—the invention of teenagers.

Alexander Graham Bell gave us the telephone. Teenagers took us one step further. They gave us the busy signal!

JOB HUNTERS

If you're going job hunting, an M.B.A. makes a good decoy.

There's a spirit of truthfulness in today's job applicants that's really refreshing. I asked one applicant if he was familiar with any machines. He said, "Four." I said, "That's great. What are the four machines?" He said, "Coke, coffee, candy, and cigarette."

I asked one job applicant what he could do and he said, "Nothing." I didn't hire him. If there's one thing I hate it's somebody who's after my job.

Have you noticed that job seekers tend to be more candid than in years gone by? We have an application that says: STATE LAST POSITION. One of the answers was: MISSIONARY.

It's wrong to say that kids aren't aware of the realities of life. My teenager went out to look for a job and it was kind of touching watching him trying to put a shine on his sneakers.

Some kids are very independent. One graduate was offered a job as a teller in a bank. He said, "I don't do windows."

JOBS

All I can say to any woman who leaves the comfort of her home to commute three hours a day in bumper-to-bumper traffic jams so she can put in ten hours a day at a nerve-racking, ulcer-producing, high-tension executive job is: "You've come a wrong way, baby!"

A lot of people are finding that even two jobs aren't enough. There's even a song about it: "I Was Failing Along on Moonlight Pay."

I'll say one thing for this job: not only does it give you a pension, but it also helps you to age a lot faster.

What can you really say about a job? To me, work will always be the fast food in the banquet of life.

Absenteeism is when people who aren't married to their jobs don't even make conjugal visits.

Have you noticed, when you get into a cab these days, the first thing you see is a half-dozen homemade signs: THANK YOU FOR NOT SMOKING. NO CHANGE MADE FOR BILLS OVER $5.00. DO NOT SLAM DOOR. DO NOT LITTER FLOOR. DO NOT OPEN WINDOW WHILE AIR CONDITIONING IS ON. Years ago we used to have cab drivers. Now we have mothers-in-law with meters.

I like the message of that sign in a consultant's office: WE CHARGE $100 AN HOUR. IF YOU WANT BRAINS CHEAP, GO TO A BUTCHER.

We deal with a printer who has a 72-hour turnaround. After 72 hours they turn around and ask for another 72 hours.

Who can forget the immortal words of our last efficiency expert when he said, "Avoid duplication. I repeat: Avoid duplication!"

Everybody's so independent these days. For instance, I know an exterminator who doesn't make house calls. . . . You ever try to put 600 cockroaches in a cab?

Now I know where that expression "the movers and the shakers" came from. The movers are people who transport your furniture from place to place—and the shakers are the people who get the bill.

I know a fella who carries a card in his wallet reading: I AM A SAFETY EXPERT. IN CASE OF ACCIDENT—SHHHH!

I was one of those nervous soldiers. When I stood guard duty, I always said, "Halt! Who went there?"

———————— has always had an interest in technology. His very first job was selling prescription windows to nearsighted Peeping Toms.

JOGGING

Jogging is when you run and you run and you run and you don't go anyplace. They got the idea from Harold Stassen!

Mark my words, jogging is unnatural. If God had meant us to run five miles every day He would have given us radial toes!

The problem with jogging is, after it's over, there's no way you can share it with other people. I mean, how do you bronze a blister?

Our neighbor just had a terrible experience. She jogged backward and gained fourteen pounds!

JOGGERS ARE NOT TO BE SNIFFED AT!

LAS VEGAS

Las Vegas is really far out. Where else can you go into a funeral parlor and see waterbed coffins?

Las Vegas is getting so expensive, the only people who can afford it are millionaires and TV repairmen. . . . Or am I repeating myself?

The first thing you notice about Las Vegas is—none of the casinos have windows. No matter what casino you go to, you get the feeling the architect majored in Basement.

Las Vegas is where a performer arrives with a director, an arranger, a conductor, a vocal coach, a writer, a manager—and then sings, "I Gotta Be Me!"

Have you noticed that Las Vegas has gone political? It's the first time I ever saw a slot machine with three lemons——————, ——————, and ——————. (FILL IN YOUR OWN CANDIDATES.)

Then there's the TV news show in Las Vegas that starts off with: "It's ten o'clock. Do you know where your bankroll is?"

All you really need to be happy in Las Vegas is a jug of wine, a loaf of bread, and thou. And then another thou. And then another thou. And then another thou.

I don't wanna complain, but every time I go to Las Vegas I feel like the Bluebird of Happiness—and every time I come back I'm a dead pigeon!

My uncle is making a fortune selling those DRIVER DOES NOT CARRY CASH signs. He sells them to deliverymen, bus drivers, and tourists leaving Las Vegas.

There's a reason why most charter flights to Las Vegas are for four days: one for the money; two for the show; three to get ready; and four to send home for more money.

LAWYERS

I read that new lawyers are being offered as much as $50,000 a year by New York law firms. It's ridiculous. When you're fresh out of law school you don't even file legal briefs. They're more like legal diapers.

You can always tell a law school graduate who starts off at $50,000 by little things. Like, his parents write *him* for money.

A photographer at a dinner for lawyers came up with a unique way of getting them to smile. He said, "Say fees!"

But I think we should all be very grateful for lawyers. Lawyers are the people who get us out of all of the trouble we never would have gotten into if it hadn't been for lawyers.

LOS ANGELES

Los Angeles is where the girls are easy on the eyes and the air isn't.

Los Angeles is really something special. It's the only town in America that offers industrial-strength air.

Who can ever forget that magic moment during the last smog attack, when 3 million people linked arms in Los Angeles and sang: "We Shall Be Overcome!"

Los Angeles is the only city I know that uses Wite-Out on air.

I just read an interesting medical statistic—that last year 30,000 people got airsick. Two hundred were in planes and the rest were in Los Angeles.

Believe me, it takes guts to cross a street in Los Angeles. This is the only town where front bumpers know karate!

There are so many wild drivers in Los Angeles, we even have a place where they get together—Forest Lawn!

MARRIAGE

Kids are right. There is absolutely nothing wrong with trial marriages. It's the trial babies that are the problem.

But it's nice to see a continuity of purpose. The student leaders of the sixties are now married, with a home in the suburbs, a mortgage, three kids—and that same intensity that used to be applied to getting out of Vietnam is now directed toward getting into the bathroom.

We happen to be very compatible. Last night I got home and my wife asked me how it went at the office with the new sales manager, with the increased quotas, and with my biggest account canceling. I said, "Great!" and she checked to see if there was liquor on my breath. Then I asked her how it had gone at home with the three kids, the sick cat, and the broken washing machine. She said, "Fantastic!" and I checked to see if there was Valium on her breath.

A good marriage is when you say, "How do I love thee, let me count the ways"—and you reach for a calculator.

Every marriage consists of a husband who comes up with a bright idea, kids who say it can't be done, and a wife who does it.

Who are we kidding? A husband controls his wife like a barometer controls the weather!

I never realized I was henpecked until last night when I heard my wife come out of our three-year-old's room saying: "Now close your eyes, go to sleep, and if you want a glass of water in the middle of the night, just call Mommy—and she'll tell Daddy."

Ten years ago my wife started wearing blue jeans and I bought a Honda. Five years ago she dyed her hair blond and I took vitamin E shots. Last month she got a face-lift and I got a transplant. And that's the way it's been through the years. Just the two of us, side by side, growing young together.

> A twenty-fourth anniversary
> Should be observed, and yet
> It's a little too early to celebrate—
> But a lot too late to regret.

Have you noticed how women are never satisfied? One wife claims she finally figured out why it's called a "silver wedding anniversary." If she wants anything she has to ask for it twenty-five times.

Then there's the auto mechanic who celebrated his twenty-fifth wedding anniversary by taking his wife on a second honeymoon. And everything went fine until he tried to return the worn-out parts.

Sometimes banking problems are in the eyes of the beholder. For instance, when it comes to our checking account, I say my wife is overdrawn. She says I'm underdeposited.

Remember when a girl would say, "You won't respect me in the morning." So you married her, carried her over the threshold and she took off her eyelashes, her eye shadow, her lipstick, her wig, her padded bra, and her girdle—but you did respect her in the morning. You just didn't recognize her.

Psychiatrists say that husbands should always be on the alert for subtle incidents that may suggest a wife's dissatisfaction—like when she vacuums your stamp collection.

A study showed that the average husband and wife only talk to each other twenty-seven minutes a week. Of course. How long does it take to say, "Uh-huh"?

If you really want to bug your wife, don't argue with her. Wait till washday, find her box of detergent, pour the powder out—and raspberry Jell-O in!

February is a very difficult month. The football season is over and the baseball season hasn't begun. What do you use to ignore your wife?

You know the marriage didn't work out when the thank-you notes for the presents are signed by a lawyer.

This is the kind of weather that makes people do strange things. I know one couple who are only staying together for the sake of the air conditioning.

The biggest problem in a divorce settlement is the wife explaining to her kids why they don't see Daddy anymore. And then the father explaining to his creditors why they don't see Money anymore.

I believe in human rights. I can't stand to see anyone deprived of them. That's why I never go to weddings.

MASSAGE PARLORS

Modern merchandising can be carried to extremes. For instance, I know a fella who made $100,000 on a self-service supermarket. Then he made $200,000 on a self-service gas station. Then he made $300,000 on a self-service restaurant. Then he lost everything. Opened a self-service massage parlor.

Sometimes you can get rich by taking a proven merchandising technique from one field and moving it to another. For instance, look at the way supermarkets sell things Mix or Match. Can you imagine what that would do for a massage parlor?

I come from a very law-abiding community. Where else have you ever seen a massage parlor with unit pricing?

You just can't equate romance with massage parlors. It's the difference between homemade and store-bought.

MEAT PRICES

Remember the good old days when we gave up meat for Lent instead of for good?

I just went to a formal dinner that served scrambled eggs. Thanks to beef prices, "It's not just for breakfast anymore."

> Mary had a little lamb.
> Before the price went up, she had a lot.

Dollar-a-pound steak is still available. All it requires is a slightly different place setting—spoon, fork, and chain saw.

I just figured out why cattle ranchers ride tall in the saddle. They sit on their wallets.

Isn't it terrible the way people try to take advantage of high beef prices? I know a farmer who's trying to teach his pigs to say, "Mooo!"

I stopped complaining about the price of beef when I realized we have a kid in college who's costing us $135 a pound.

MEDICINE

I happen to be a very chicken patient. I get an ingrown toenail and the next day I'm buying a ticket to Lourdes.

Once upon a time a patient went into a Medicaid clinic and got a blood test, a blood pressure test, an eye test, a urine analysis, X rays, an electrocardiogram, and a brain scan—but it didn't work out. When he left his hangnail was as bad as ever.

I really haven't kept up with new developments in medicine. I still think the Heimlich Maneuver is something you use on girls named Heimlich.

If medical science has done so much to add years to our lives, how come you never meet a woman who's past forty?

MEETINGS

I'm always concerned when a dinner meeting begins with a prayer. I'm never quite sure if the Program Chairman has seen the light or the entree.

Sometimes I wonder if we shouldn't reverse the order of these meetings. We say a prayer and then we hear the Treasurer's Report. Maybe it should be the other way around.

To emphasize the festive mood of this occasion, we're going to accentuate the positive and eliminate the negative. Therefore, the prayer will be lengthened—and the Treasurer's Report will be omitted.

The worst job you can have in any organization is Treasurer—because, no matter what is proposed, you have to think of it in terms of money. I'm firmly convinced that if our Treasurer had arranged for the Last Supper—there would have been a cash bar.

> In any given meeting,
> When all is said and done;
> 90% will be said—
> 10% will be done.

I just hope I'm adequately prepared for this very important occasion. Standing here tonight, I feel a little like Moses with two tablets of stone and a ballpoint pen.

The meeting will now come to order. Or, to use the generic term, SHUT UP!

MEN

God must have meant males to be the superior sex. Why else would we end every prayer with "Ah! Men!"

I try to be very humble about this, but I once applied for a job as a model for *Playgirl* magazine—but they said I was overqualified.

Last week I went to the beach, I flexed my powerful biceps, and one girl was amazed. She said, "Why, you've got muscles like potatoes!" I said, "Idaho?" She said, "Mashed!"

I hate comparisons. I keep telling myself that Robert Redford is a mirage.

Beards are still very popular. At least I think they're beards. They're either beards or all that fiber in our diets is backing up.

Conservative? It's the first time I ever saw a pin-striped toga.

Some people are naturally cautious. For instance, my uncle was fitted with a pacemaker and ever since he's worn a string tie. Well, it really isn't a string tie. What it is, is jumper cables.

You'll have to excuse him. He's going through a nonentity crisis.

I wouldn't say he's dumb but I think he majored in "Huh?"

I didn't say he was a liar. I just said that when he tells the truth it has stretch marks.

I didn't say he was a liar. I just said if you ask him for an honest answer he puts it on back order.

MEXICO

People are wondering if all that oil down there has changed our attitude toward Mexico. In a word, *sí*.

They say that Mexico may have as much as 200 billion barrels of oil and I believe it. It's the first time I ever saw a wetback make it and a Texan dry him off.

Mexico also has enormous reserves of natural gas. It's found in three principal locations—tamales, enchiladas, and burritos.

MIDDLE AGE

I've reached that stage in life where I know where it's at—but it's a little farther than I want to go.

I'm at that age where I get discouraged by little things. Like a kid calling his father "the old man"—and Dad is thirty-two.

Nostalgia is always relative to the age of the nostalgee. If you're middle-aged, you look at a plastic Christmas tree and remember back to when they were the real thing—aluminum!

> Middle age is when your glasses and your waistline get
>   thicker,
> And your hair and your wallet get thinner;
> When you don't give much thought to exercise—
> And entirely too much to dinner.

Every time I look in a mirror I find it increasingly hard to accept the fact that we were created in God's image. I just can't see God as being fat, fifty, and wearing bifocals.

Nature is merciful. It makes us wear bifocals so we won't be able to read the numbers on our bathroom scales.

When my optometrist fitted me for bifocals, the first thing he warned me about is the Dolly Parton syndrome—seeing stairs can be a problem.

At twenty, you want to be the master of your fate and the captain of your soul. At fifty, you're inclined to settle for being the master of your weight and the captain of your bowling team.

I said, "Doc, I don't wanna brag, but I can do the same thing at fifty I did at twenty!" He said, "What's that?" I said, "Lie!"

The more I read about the rising cost of college tuition, the trauma of making career decisions, the emotional stresses created by the new sexual freedom, social permissiveness, and the drug scene—the more I'm tempted to say, "T.G.I.F. Thank God I'm Fifty!"

Middle age is when skintight isn't that accurate a description.

Incidentally, when you get up in the morning and you look at your face in the bathroom mirror—I just discovered a wonderful way to eliminate wrinkles. Take off your glasses!

What the middle-aged of America really need isn't jogging, dieting, exercises, or face-lifts—just younger mirrors.

I've come to the reluctant conclusion that either I'm getting wrinkles or my skin is turning to corduroy!

People say they don't have wrinkles, they have laugh lines. We must do a lot more laughing after forty.

When you're over fifty you have good news and bad news. The bad news is, you can no longer understand the lyrics to popular songs. The good news is, you can no longer understand the lyrics to popular songs.

Being fifty-five is like driving 55—everybody seems to pass you.

I've reached the age where I'm very concerned with physical comfort. I mean, I have an electric blanket I'm remembering in my will.

I love my comfort. I'm not going to retire to Florida until La-Z-Boy makes beach chairs.

Every day of our life offers a fresh start. I'm not forty-nine years old. I'm forty-nine years new!

MIDDLE EAST

You know what would add another very interesting dimension to the Mideast problem? If somebody invented a car that ran on chicken soup.

These are not easy times for the Prime Minister of Israel. I understand he has three trays on his desk: IN, OUT, and DON'T ASK.

Peace in the Middle East would be fantastic. This is the only area of the world where they have wall samplers that read LOVE THY NEIGHBOR—immediately followed by six paragraphs of small print.

Sometimes you have an agreement and then the only remaining problem is to agree on what the agreement everybody agreed to agreed to.

MONEY

Every time I look at my ten-room house, my new Cadillac, my three kids in Ivy League colleges, and my wife standing there in her full-length mink coat—I can't help but take a reflective puff on my Corona Corona cigar and think: "Why shouldn't I be $200,000 in debt?"

The only way to survive in today's business world is to have an M.B.A.—a Massive Bank Account.

The national debt now stands at well over a trillion dollars. I've heard of overdrafts, but this is ridiculous.

I'm not against all government spending—but does the Washington Monument really need aluminum siding?

Last week I spent $500 to fly out to California, $100 to rent a car, $30 for gas to drive to a $150-a-day resort to attend a $395 seminar entitled: MONEY ISN'T EVERYTHING.

The biggest problem facing America today is the money supply. You get home and the first thing your family says is: "Money! Supply!"

Let's keep our perspective on this. Sure, gold is selling for more than $————— an ounce—but is it happy?

I wish they wouldn't put IN GOD WE TRUST on our money. I'm always afraid that someday I'll be praying: "Our Father who art in Chapter Eleven!"

They say "money talks." Unfortunately, when it hears my name it says, "Who?"

If money is a curse, my wallet is rated G.

What this country really needs is a pacemaker for pocketbooks.

We're living in an age of pocket calculators and nothing in our pockets to calculate.

Growing up is that slow, painful transition from praying that your face will clear to praying that your check will clear.

Have you noticed that, when money flies, it never goes Economy Class?

Today Opportunity knocked on my door—and asked how to get to the Rockefellers.

For those of you who have been saving your money for a rainy day —welcome to the monsoon season.

It's incredible. They now have a roller coaster that makes a complete loop and people go around this loop with their hands held over their heads. I still can't decide if they're brave or trying to catch change.

"The love of money is the root of all evil." That's why I don't want to love it—I just want to live with it.

MOTHER'S DAY

If you're one of five kids and you really want to give your mom a present that will please her like all get out—all get out.

Tell me, does anybody really know that mothers like candy, carnations, and potted plants? Thanks to Mother's Day, the unhappiest people on earth are overweight mothers with hay fever!

Our local florist talks to plants. What does he say? "Don't die before Mother's Day! Please don't die before Mother's Day!"

A lot of people have given up flowers as a Mother's Day gift because of the health problem. They've proven conclusively that three dozen long-stemmed roses causes poverty in laboratory mice.

Mother's Day is the cleanest day of the year. After dinner the kids sit Mom in a chair and wash all the pots, pans, cutlery, and dishes. They leave. Mom makes sure they're gone. Then she washes all the pots, pans, cutlery, and dishes.

MOVIES

Hollywood is now making an updated version of the Bible. You can tell it's an updated version because Moses comes down from Mount Sinai, reads the Ten Commandments, and then says, "Coming up, sports and the weather!"

King Kong has been an awe-inspiring figure for people all over the country except for certain neighborhoods in Chicago where he's considered effeminate.

King Kong looks like a chimpanzee built on a cost-plus government contract.

Have you noticed how popular the word "killer" has become? There are movies about killer bees, killer earthquakes, killer sharks. Now there's a new movie that'll strike fear into the heart of every housewife—*Killer Dust!*

> I saw *Gone With the Wind* again,
> But a new era now has dawned;
> I know it 'cause during that famous scene—
> When Rhett said "damn," I yawned.

I never realized how popular camping had become until a theater ran an old Lon Chaney movie and called it *The Backpacker of Notre Dame*.

> Breathes there a film buff who hasn't grown picky,
> At the floors of theaters, so cruddy and sticky?
> You hope for the best, but you know in a flash:
> On the floor and the screen—is nothing but trash.

When it comes to the behavior of audiences at drive-in movies, I try not to be a prude. I feel that whatever goes on between a man and a woman in the privacy of their own motorcycle is their business.

I don't want to brag, but I still get Saturday Night Fever. Every Saturday night I go to the movies, look at the prices, and do I get hot!

MUSIC

I'm not a big fan of music. Personally, I prefer the Mormon Tabernacle Quiet.

I love cowboy songs. Show me a man who sings, "Yippee-ay-o-tie-a, yippee-ay-a-tie-oh," and I'll show you a fella who's forgotten the lyrics!

You don't realize how hip the world is getting until you see a Salvation Army band reading *Variety*.

> The inconsistencies of life
> Must really reach a height
> When a hundred-and-fifty-five-piece brass band
> Goes out and plays "Silent Night!"

You really have to admire the string section of the (SNOWBOUND CITY) Symphony Orchestra in this weather. It's the first time I ever heard Beethoven's Fifth played with mittens.

Anyone who says that "nothing could be finer than to be in Carolina in the morning"—has lived a very sheltered life.

Television is all heart. I understand that next year they're going to do an updated version of "The Little Drummer Boy"—this time with bongos.

I don't know what this world is coming to. They now have an X-rated opera. Features the world's first off-coloratura soprano.

My hobby is writing songs. In fact, yesterday I ran over to my neighbor and I said, "I did it! I did it! I just finished writing a sympathy!" He said, "You mean symphony. Sympathy is when you feel sorry for something." I said, "Wait'll you hear it!"

We're just not a militaristic nation. You can see it in parades. In what other countries do you hear marching bands playing Cole Porter?

Marching bands are musical organizations that move very fast—and once you hear them, you know why.

Marching bands have pioneered a brand-new concept in the performing arts—no-fault melody.

I heard one band that was just fantastic. No matter what they played, the cymbals carried the melody.

Barbershop quartets tend to follow a pattern. There is always one very fat fella—who sings tenor. One very skinny fella—who sings bass. And two others who always have their arms outstretched and their hands open. You're never quite sure if they're reaching for a note or a beer.

A barbershop quartet is where melody is hiding out until rock and roll blows over.

I always get confused by the grammar of popular songs. I can never remember if OH YEAH comes before DOO WAH or after OO OO EE!

NATIONAL PARKS

My son got a summer job as a park ranger, which is nothing short of amazing. He wouldn't know the Grand Canyon from a hole in the ground.

A New Yorker was flying to Los Angeles and when the airliner reached Arizona the announcement was made that they were now passing over the Grand Canyon. He looked down for a few seconds and then went back to his magazine. The stewardess said, "You don't seem too impressed." The New Yorker said, "You've seen one pothole, you've seen them all!"

I always enjoy visiting South Dakota—where Rushmore is a mountain and not a requirement.

We visited Mount Rushmore in the fall and an early snowfall had flecked old Abe's hair and beard with white. As we stared up at the awe-inspiring sight, my wife nudged me, leaned over, and whispered, "Did you remember to pack your Grecian Formula?"

NEIGHBORS

Our neighbors have eight kids and it's always interesting to see them in a supermarket. They have a riding shopping cart.

My neighbor is very upset about school busing. He thinks they ought to leave schools where they are.

Our neighbors are really a fun couple. She spends all her time dolling up and he spends all his time jogging. We call them Sweety and Sweaty!

It isn't hard to be a good neighbor. All you have to be is three things: friendly, alert, and live next door to a nudist camp!

> The presidential debate will be thrilling,
> But the greatest debates of them all
> Are the ones you have to listen to—
> With your ear against the wall!

Our neighbors are going through a midlife crisis. She claims he hasn't shown any life in his mid in months.

I feel sorry for my neighbor's wife. Last weekend he watched the World Series on one TV set and the football games on another. The only time she got to talk to him was when the seventh-inning stretch came at halftime!

My neighbor spends every weekend of the fall and winter watching football on TV. That's all he lives for—football on TV. For four months out of every year, sex is a naked reverse!

We had a fantastic Sunday. A fella down the block invited the entire neighborhood over for a barbecue of prime sirloins, T-bones, and filet mignons. It just shows you what can happen when a person's heart opens up and his freezer breaks down.

I'll say one thing for our neighbors: they're generous. It's just wonderful the way they're always willing to share their appetite with our barbecue.

NEWS

When are they going to start writing newspapers with a happy ending?

If the truth be known—your town has a pretty good newspaper.

I once considered building a tree house. It's the only way I could think of to have the kid who delivers our paper hit the front door.

It always upsets me to read the obituary page. If you go by the pictures, they all look so healthy!

In a way, a news update is like a quickie. It's a real good idea but done too fast.

News updates on television are fine, but what this country really needs are news backdates. A story that America is the most powerful nation in the world. A report that America has the strongest economy in the world. A late-breaking item that the American dollar has reached new highs throughout the world. And then the commercial—for a $2000 Chevy.

NEW YEAR'S EVE

An astrologer just gave me some bad news. She said, "Beware of any year that begins with 19."

Life is like a New Year's Eve party. There's a very old man and a very young baby—and all those in between are paying the bills.

One New Year's Eve I stood up at our local pub and said it was time to get ready. At the stroke of midnight, I wanted every husband to be standing next to the one person who made his life worth living. Well, it was kind of embarrassing. The bartender was almost crushed to death.

I always get carried away on New Year's Eve. One year, at the stroke of midnight, I grabbed the person next to me and kissed and kissed and kissed! I'll never forget it. Neither will that waiter.

Personally, I prefer to have bad weather on New Year's Eve. I hate it when the barometer's steady and I'm not.

There's a reason why, on New Year's Eve, they always refer to it as the "stroke of midnight." When you get the bill that's what you have.

And every New Year's Day someone comes in while you're sleeping and leaves a tremendous hangover under your cranium. It's the Toot Fairy!

As we begin the new year, there is good news and bad news. The good news is, we have finally reached (YEAR). The bad news is, it's the bottom line of our heating bill.

Force of habit is an interesting thing. Here it is January and I keep writing (PREVIOUS YEAR) on the bank's checks—and they keep writing INSUFFICIENT FUNDS on mine.

It's January 10th. Do you know where your New Year's resolutions are?

NEW YORK

My wife has come up with the only way to keep New York City clean. Slipcovers! One end fits over Staten Island and the other over the Bronx.

They've got to do something about cleaning up Times Square. Right now it's more like "Give My Discards to Broadway."

Sometimes truth is funnier than fiction. On a recent trip to the big city the train conductor announced, "In three minutes we will arrive in New York City. Watch your step as you leave the train!"

I once knew a fella who was born in Texas, raised in California, got his education in Massachusetts, became a junior executive in Illinois, a senior executive in Ohio, president of a corporation in Pennsylvania, spent his retirement in New York City, died, and went to hell. And you know something? The change had been so gradual, he never noticed the difference.

We shouldn't panic about the future because at this very moment there are 12,000 people who have all the answers to America's problems. Five are candidates and the rest are driving cabs in New York.

NUCLEAR POWER

A Princeton University laboratory ran a fusion test that achieved a temperature of 60 million degrees! Do you realize what a temperature of 60 million degrees could lead to? For the first time in history, room service will be able to deliver coffee while it's still hot!

Nobody can be sure what long-term effect nuclear radiation has on people. For instance, my Uncle Willie worked in a nuclear power plant for fifteen years, put in for early retirement, and just last week started a second career in Portland, Maine—as a lighthouse.

Fortunately there are always telltale little signs when you are exposed to radiation. For instance, your pocket calculator no longer runs on batteries—it runs on you!

Regulatory authorities, utility executives, and nuclear experts all join together to issue a statement explaining what really happened when there's a nuclear plant accident—but is "Ooops" enough?

Needless to say, we've learned some very important lessons from nuclear accidents. For instance, all traffic signs within a ten-mile radius of a nuclear power plant will now say WALK and RUN LIKE HELL.

You can always tell when a nuclear power plant reaches the danger point. It's when they move the billing department to a safer location.

I'd like to dedicate this next song to the nuclear power industry: "Warning Bells Are Breaking up That Old Gang of Mine."

Now I know why nuclear generators are called fail-safe. They're safe right up until they fail.

I think it's great the way the scientists and the environmentalists have finally reached a compromise. They're going to build the world's first 10-million-kilowatt nuclear-powered candle.

You just can't argue with that sign that says: A NUCLEAR HOLOCAUST COULD RUIN YOUR WHOLE DAY.

OFFICE WORK

Happiness is an unlisted IN basket.

Happiness is a very small desk and a very big wastebasket.

Keeping the top of your desk neat is easy. All it requires is diligence, organization, and twenty-six drawers.

I guess it's all in the way you look at it. The boss calls it a compact office. I call it a walk-in desk.

Whenever I get a note FROM THE DESK OF—I let my drapes answer it.

Office politics is nothing but quibbling rivalry.

Bad taste is putting someone who stutters in charge of the Xerox machine.

As an office worker, I've always wanted to have a job in the Vatican. The pay isn't so good but they never take up a collection for weddings or babies.

Believe me, business should only be as good as office collections. Last week I contributed to five babies, four weddings, three birthdays, and two people leaving. It's ridiculous. I know one woman who hit the jackpot—$8000! She resigned on her birthday when she had a baby while getting married!

This is the kind of weather where you wake up, look out at the snowdrifts, reach for the phone, dial your office, and call in warm.

I'll never forget how I met my secretary. It was in a stationery store. It's the first time I ever saw anybody buy a six-pack of correction fluid.

You can't blame the average secretary for being discouraged when she realizes that six months of her life will be spent on HOLD.

Any executive who plays around with his secretary, the file clerk, and the receptionist should do one of two things—get married or get divorced.

One good thing about office parties—you catch up on what's happening. I went over to the receptionist and I said, "Congratulations. I hear you and George got married. We all thought he was just fooling around." She said, "So did George."

We had a rather emotional morning in our office today—tears, cries of anguish, gnashing of teeth—and it's all because of our postman, the late John Doe. He didn't die. He's just late.

I don't want to complain about delivery, but at least parcel post is a very honest name. Parcel is a package and a post is something that doesn't move.

If the White House is serious about making food a weapon, our company cafeteria could be another Manhattan Project.

It's really unique. I still can't figure out how they can get everything to turn green but the spinach.

I have one of those factory-second beepers. When I get a message, it doesn't make a noise but the garage doors go up.

Beepers are a symptom of our time. It used to be that you filled a briefcase with work so you could bring your office home with you. Thanks to beepers, now you can bring the switchboard too.

A coffee break is the first rest of the day of your life.

OIL

We have reached the eeny, meeny, miney stage of oil because pretty soon there ain't gonna be no mo!

It's so exasperating. They say there's only enough oil in the world to last another fifty years. Well, don't just stand there—plant more!

Somehow I'm never quite sure if "crude" refers to the oil or the pricing.

There is no justice in this world. A tanker can spill 6 million barrels of oil and nothing happens. Your kid spills a glass of milk and you hit him.

You think we're having trouble now with all those tankers bringing in oil? What if it were mailed in?

No matter what happens to the price of oil, you know who's going to pay for it. Every utility in the country has its customers by the bills.

Heating oil dealers must love the poor. They've made so many of them.

OLD AGE

I love it when people say, "You're not getting older, you're just getting better." I have one problem with that. The only thing I seem to be getting better at—is getting older.

Life is nothing but snap, crackle, and pop. When you're young, it's cereal. When you're old, it's joints.

Life is unfair. We spend the first half of our lives crossing our fingers that we won't get arthritis—and the second half not crossing our fingers because we got arthritis.

I admire people who can plan ahead. So far the only thing I have put aside for my old age is arthritis, gout, and high blood pressure.

I'm at that age where a miracle cure is anything that's paid for by Medicare.

I go back to the days of the Fortune 500—when, if you had 500, it was a fortune!

Growing older is an entirely new learning experience. It's when you first realize that Polident is not a damaged parrot.

An old-timer is someone who remembers when telephone cords were kinky and sex wasn't.

Temperature is always a problem in Sun City. You're never quite sure which is going to win out—the cool from the air conditioning or the heat from the birthday cakes.

> My posture was like an exclamation point:
> "Stand straight and tall," said Momma.
> But then the years just took their toll—
> I now stand like a comma.

I think my doctor is giving up on my circulation. He says the only thing that will help is pardoning of the arteries.

One sure sign that you're having trouble with your teeth is when they have to marinate your Jell-O.

I'm at that age where I have to find my hearing aid to ask where my glasses are.

My grandfather always claimed it was evident to him that Adam and Eve in the Garden of Eden were very young. He said, "When you're my age, just biting into the apple would have been punishment enough."

I'm at that age where I'm beginning to wonder if my sex drive was taken over by the post office. Sometimes it takes me five days to deliver.

A senior citizen was telling me that when you reach seventy there's still good news and bad news. The good news is, you still have lust in your heart. The bad news is, you have rust everywhere else.

I won't say how old he is but he celebrated his last birthday with a cake that had one candle for every year. It's the first time I ever saw anybody blow out a birthday cake with asbestos lips.

Have you noticed that as you grow older you become more and more like Xerox? You keep repeating yourself.

OPERATIONS

You know something that has always bothered me about hospitals? You pay a top-notch, world-renowned surgeon $10,000 to operate—but the minute you go under the anesthetic, you don't know who's cutting you open. It could be a Boy Scout who's getting his Merit Badge in Appendectomy.

I go to a very courteous hospital. They even have a sign in the operating room: THANK YOU FOR NOT CROAKING.

For the first few days after an operation you suffer from bridge-table legs. They keep folding up under you.

I wish people wouldn't ask me about my operation—particularly when they have only an hour to spare.

OPTIMISM

The good news is that the world's future is pregnant with possibilities. The bad news is, it's now in its 8,947,548th month.

In Alaska, an optimist is anyone who owns a motorcycle with a heater.

Optimism is going into a real estate broker's office and saying, "I'd like to see something in a four-bedroom, three-bath house for $16,000—me!"

I'm an optimist. I figure, if it was really a dog-eat-dog world, they wouldn't be selling so much Alpo.

Optimism is holding firm to the belief that you're not unpopular. It's just that your telephone answering machine is.

Optimism is thinking the E in your gas gauge stands for ENOUGH.

OVERWEIGHT

Now here's the problem: 3000 dietitians are helping Americans to lose weight—and 3 million bakers are helping them find it.

My wife is very sensitive about her weight. How do you explain to her she caught pneumonia from standing in front of an open refrigerator?

Overweight is when you go to empty your pockets—and they are.

No use talking, I've got to lose some weight. Yesterday I had to let my toga out.

I find that I get very disagreeable when I gain weight. Very disagreeable. They don't call me Attila the Ton for nothing.

Fat? If I wanted to let it all hang out, it would take two trips!

PERSONALITIES

After all the troubles I've had to cope with this week, all I can say is, "T.G.I.F. Thank God I'm Fantastic!"

If there's anything to Darwin's theory of evolution, in the future some people are going to have one ear and two mouths.

Institutions are a lot easier to deal with than people. Stores and offices have a closing time—mouths don't.

People fall into three distinct categories. There are those who light a candle and there are those who curse the darkness. Then there are the others who light a candle, burn themselves, and then curse both the candle and the darkness.

I'm always wary of pious people who say mean things about others. It reminds me that three types of people put their arms around you—friends, lovers, and muggers.

I make it a point never to repeat gossip. So please listen good the first time.

A gossip is someone who retails details.

Conceit is when there's a flash of lightning and you say: "Please, no pictures!"

My uncle's a nudist. He feels that when it comes to leisure suits—nothing beats *you!*

Some people are consumed by ambition. In my case, ambition never had that much of an appetite.

It's terrible to be indecisive. I always feel like a centipede who's been told to put his best foot forward.

I make it a practice never to take notes. If there's one thing I hate, it's a memo pad that's smarter than I am.

You can always tell people who put their foot in their mouth by little things. Like their toothpaste is from Dr. Scholl.

I always thought I had big feet. For years I was obsessed with the idea that I had the biggest feet in the world. Everywhere I went I thought people were staring at my big feet. Finally I went to a psychiatrist. I spent three years and $25,000 and he finally convinced me I did not have big feet. So I went to a fancy restaurant to celebrate and I asked to be shown to the best table they had. The maître d' said, "Of course. But you'll have to take off your skis first."

I happen to be very gullible. Last year I invested $5000 in a solar darkroom.

A neurotic is someone who's self-employed and doesn't get along with his boss.

Look at the bright side of being nervous. How much cholesterol is there in fingernails?

The best way to deal with an exhibitionist is to be sympathetic. Just say, "I don't blame you for being upset. Maybe Ralph Nader could get you another one!"

Fortunately, I don't believe in superstitions like Friday the thirteenth—knock wood.

It doesn't pay to be nice to people. It really doesn't. I was at a P.T.A. meeting last night when a mother came in late, apologized and said, "I've been having a lot of trouble with my sitter." And I said, "I know how you feel. I have hemorrhoids myself."

PESSIMISM

You think you have troubles. An astrologer just told me the twentieth is my unlucky century.

Today is the tomorrow you worried about yesterday—but not nearly enough.

A pessimist is an optimist who has just heard the Dow Jones closing.

A pessimist is someone who thinks that God created the world in six days—and on the seventh day He was laid off.

A pessimist is an optimist who read the 10-K.

A pessimist is an optimist on the way back.

Pessimism is contagious. You get it from standing too close to the Seven O'Clock News.

My neighbor carries a little card in his wallet. It says: I AM A PESSIMIST. IN CASE OF ACCIDENT, I'M NOT SURPRISED.

Do you ever get the feeling your life cycle has a flat tire?

Did you ever get the feeling you were born under a ladder?

I've never been lucky. Remember when millions of people were looking up and saying, "Is it a bird? Is it a plane? It's Superman!" Every time I looked up—it was a bird.

I'm so unlucky, I would have had a singles club on Noah's Ark.

I'm so unlucky, if I were born again, I'd get another bill from the obstetrician.

It's a waste of time to tell people to go to hell. Nowadays, hell delivers.

All my life I've waited for a sign that would lead me to fame, fortune, power, and the adulation of all mankind—a sign that would allow me to scale the uppermost heights of human achievement. And this morning I saw that sign. It said: AUTHORIZED PERSONNEL ONLY.

Life is just a bowl of cherries—a little more expensive than you can afford.

PETS

There are three types of fish that can very quickly do you in: a shark, a barracuda, and a guppy that's part of a starter aquarium kit.

I figure that our goldfish has now cost us $185 an ounce. I don't know whether to feed him or have him set in a ring.

You know what bothers me about the palimony decisions? They establish the precedent that, if someone lives with you for a few years, they're entitled to a settlement. And I can't tell you what problems this is going to create. Like my goldfish just hired a lawyer.

I have the most frustrated pet in the world. It's a turtle that chases cars!

PHILOSOPHY

Blessed are the trite, for they shall insipid the earth.

"Today is the first day of the rest of your life." Unless you live on the other side of the international date line, in which case, yesterday was the first day of the rest of your life.

Someday each one of us is going to be over the hill. Our job in life is to make sure that hill is a big one.

A lot of people drink at the Fountain of Knowledge, but very few of them ever suffer from edema.

Some people think our best years are those between adolescence and middle age—when we've finished our preparation for life and haven't quite begun our preparation for H.

Live your life so that if someone says, "Be yourself," it's good advice.

The world may owe you a living but you have to do the repossessing.

Motivation is when your dreams put on work clothes.

Instinct is the triumph of mind over data.

I wish people wouldn't keep saying, "The proof is in the pudding." It's like one day I'll be eating dessert and I'll find eighteen and a half minutes of tape.

Sometimes I think all the poetry has gone out of our lives. Two centuries ago Lord Byron could say, "Roll on, thou deep and dark blue ocean!" Today the only thing we have that rolls on is deodorants.

Routine is what makes the world go flat.

Smart is when you only believe half of what you hear. Brilliant is when you know which half.

There are no simple answers. Simple answerers, yes.

Second opinions are very popular these days. People think a second and then give you their opinion.

The only problem with jawboning is, sometimes the bone is in another part of the head.

"People learn from their mistakes." What they learn is that they should have studied more for the test.

Mistakes are the adolescence of experience.

Whoever said, "Nothing is impossible," never tried to slam a revolving door.

Never lock up advice. It's so rarely taken.

Pandora's box should have had a better lock.

The difference between good times and bad times is like the difference between ballet and modern dance. One puts you on your toes —the other sets you on your heels.

If it wasn't for hard knocks, how would you ever know opportunity was there?

The School of Experience is also an ivy-covered college—poison.

If you want to relish living,
It really is a breeze;
Be sure you smell the flowers—
But first you check for bees.

Life is too grim—with conflicts it's fraught;
Why couldn't anger be a spectator sport?

When I answer someone's anger,
I follow this to the letter:
Tongue in cheek is good;
Tongue in check is better.

I try not to be critical. I figure, let him who is without gall cast the first stones.

Life is a lot like wearing bifocals. There are two ways to look at almost anything.

People are funny, you will agree.
When dealt a blow, they say, "Why me?"
But when good luck becomes their lot—
They're quick to answer, "Well, why not?"

Sometimes I get the feeling I'm sailing through life under a flag of convenience—and it's white.

Let your conscience be your guide;
Face each crisis without a yelp.
I let conscience be my guide—
And all I can say is: "HELP!"

The one plus of wrestling with your conscience is—you're a professional and it's an amateur.

A sigh is an amplifier for people who suffer in silence.

Happiness consists of living each day as if it were the first day of your marriage and the last day of your vacation.

Live it up! When you cross the river Styx, it's exact change only—everything you have.

I think, therefore I had better thwim.

I believe in enthusiasm and involvement. Corpses are laid back.

I've been studying yoga and the very first time I assumed the lotus position I learned a great truth. I learned that my wife is right. I do have cold feet!

POLITICAL CAMPAIGNS

Nature has four principal ways of thinning out the herd: drought, famine, floods, and primaries.

It's amazing how many people are beginning to zero in on running for President. Zero being their qualifications.

The political campaigns are really picking up speed. You can tell. People are yawning much faster.

This is the time in the campaign when you begin to wonder if all political speeches weren't born under the same sign—Taurus.

The first thing you learn during a campaign speech is that Thanksgiving isn't the only time you see a turkey stuffed with chestnuts.

I love presidential campaigns. At what other time do you see people in their fifties capitalizing on their youth?

But it's heartwarming the way (FIRST LADY) is going out and giving those speeches—and I just love her slogan: HE AIN'T HEAVY. HE'S MY HUSBAND.

POLITICAL CANDIDATES

I won't say what I think of one of the candidates, but if I ever drink a toast to him, I'll use Wild Turkey.

Actually, there are many similarities between the worlds of advertising and politics. In advertising, Serutan is "natures" backward. In politics, (CANDIDATE) is everything backward.

"On a scale of ten, how do you rate (CANDIDATE)?" "Do you allow fractions?"

Some people are wondering whether one of the candidates has had a face-lift. Well, let's put it this way: he either has a face-lift or support sideburns.

You really have to admire the (POLITICAL PARTY). They now have ten candidates. One for each vote.

You can't blame (CANDIDATE) for not wanting his headquarters next to a Burger King. The signs would read: (CANDIDATE) HEADQUARTERS—HOME OF THE WHOPPER.

Everybody's talking about the way —————— got his campaign off to a flying stop.

You have to admit that —————— has the gift of gab. Unfortunately, he still hasn't opened it.

I love to hear him being interviewed. Some people want him to get his act together. I'd settle for him getting his words together.

Until I heard him extemporize, I never realized the five vowels were A, E, I, O, and UH.

POLITICAL CONVENTIONS

There's something very exciting about a political convention that's held at the peak of the summertime. It's such a thrill seeing thousands of people sticking firmly to their convictions, their candidates, and their chairs.

A political platform is like the second stanza of "The Star-Spangled Banner." Everybody knows it's there but very few know the words to it.

The best reason for choosing a candidate on the first ballot has to be $150-a-day hotel rooms.

POLITICAL DINNERS

There are two ways to survive in this world. One: never stand up in a canoe. Two: never sit down at a $1000-a-plate dinner.

It's always a thrill going to a $1000-a-plate fund-raising dinner. To look down and realize that stain on your tie cost you $18.45.

I hate to go to fund-raising barbecues. There's something about paying $100 a plate—and that plate is paper.

POLITICIANS

In 1776, 56 people signed the Declaration of Independence, separating this country from England. Today the only thing you can get 56 politicians to agree on is recess.

A politician was getting dressed to go to a fund-raising dinner when his wife exploded. She said, "It's ridiculous. Every night it's either a meeting, a reception, a banquet, or a testimonial. I think I'd drop dead on the spot if you ever spent an evening at home." He said, "Please, dear. Under the new rules we're not allowed to accept bribes."

One politician claims he's just a country boy at heart. I think the country is Oz.

I won't say how tall (SHORT CANDIDATE) is, but he could be the first candidate ever to get into the White House on his record and into movies at half price.

Fortunately, his campaign advisers are taking steps that will soon make him stand ten feet tall. Subtle things—like elevator rugs.

It's perfectly all right to shake hands with a politician—providing you count your fingers afterward.

It's bad enough when politicians are compared to used-car salesmen. What really hurts is when the used-car salesmen complain.

Politicians tend to be very humble people. They know that honesty is the best policy. They're just reluctant to take the best for themselves.

As any smart politician knows, the best position to take is one that's to the left of the Republicans, to the right of the Democrats, and to the front of the cameras.

It's always fascinating to see a politician change his position under pressure. There's even a name for it: Shake and Break!

Loyalty is the key word in Washington. There's a sign on the Cabinet table: YES SPOKEN HERE.

It always bothers me when politicians talk about an Eleventh Commandment. What makes them think God needs help?

POLITICS

Benjamin Franklin once said, "I wish the bald eagle had not been chosen as the representative of our country; he is a bird of bad moral character . . . the turkey is a much more respectable bird." And that statement has set a pattern for the many elections since— with one party running the turkeys and the other getting the bird.

I once made the mistake of buying a used car that was formerly owned by a little old lady in Chicago who only used it for going to vote. It had 114,000 miles on it.

Nowadays being a (LOSING PARTY) is a little like taking the up elevator on the *Titanic.*

I'm so naive, I thought "special interest groups" were people who got 6% mortgages.

You can always tell the procrastinators in politics. They're the ones who are trying to get up a Stop Nixon movement.

There are a lot of misconceptions about politics. For instance, they say the office makes the man—but only if it's located in a massage parlor.

Some political positions are like peanut butter. They stick to the roof of your doubt.

POLLUTION

They're really doing something about noise pollution. For instance, when was the last time you heard opportunity knock?

What bothers me is when I'm sitting in a cab that's getting 22 miles to a quart of oil and the cabby is telling me not to smoke.

I love to shake up tourists about the smog. If I see one of them eating an ice cream cone, I go up to them and say, "You want to know how dirty the air is? I'll bet you think that's chocolate!"

We went away for one of those romantic weekends at Lake Erie. Walked along the shore and collected drift garbage.

People have the darnedest problems on vacations. My neighbor got his foot stuck in Lake Erie.

Remember when Jell-O came in six different flavors and water didn't?

If we don't do something about pollution, the meek won't inherit the earth—the muck will.

We are all traveling together on this spaceship Earth. Let's not make it into a garbage scow.

POPE

The Sistine Chapel. Now that's what I call a voting booth!

I've always admired that throne the Pope is carried around on. I understand it has an E.P.A. rating of four miles per bearer in the country, two in the city.

Millions of people waited hours to see the Pope and it made a profound impression on people all over the world. In Vegas, a singer dropped two songs and added three prayers.

The Pope's travels have really had a humbling effect on reporters. I heard one of them praying: "Forgive us our press passes."

Of course the Pope did well. Look who does his material.

It must be wonderful to be the Pope. To be able to call up DIAL-A-PRAYER and ask, "Any messages?"

POSTAL RATES

When the price of postage stamps does go up, I predict there will be no public outcry—for three very good reasons: there will be greater understanding on the part of the public; there will be better service on the part of the post office; and there will be Valium in the glue.

I don't want to seem snobbish, but I have always appreciated the more expensive things in life: diamonds, Beluga caviar, Cadillacs, and postage.

—— cents to mail a letter? It's ridiculous. Nowadays who has news that good?

—— cents an ounce has a familiar ring to it. Oh yes. It's the perfume the kids buy for Mother's Day.

But —— cents an ounce should allow the post office to make some much-needed improvements. For instance, in the dead letter office, adding a grief therapist.

POST OFFICE

I firmly believe that our nation will go on for many thousands and thousands of years. We'll have to just to get all the mail delivered.

The biggest challenge facing the post office today is a medical problem. If an employee comes down with sleeping sickness, how can you tell?

The U. S. Post Office system is now over two hundred years old. If you were that old, you'd move slow too.

Do you ever get the feeling that fast, efficient, reliable mail service is an idea whose time has gone?

Did you hear about the obstetrician who decided to make a midlife career change, so he went to work for the post office? And it still took nine months to make a delivery.

There's an old saying that tomorrow never comes—but only if the post office is delivering it.

Progress is wonderful. Now you can send a letter from one city to another and the post office promises next-day delivery. It costs $——— and it's called Express Mail. I can remember when it cost three cents and it was called U. S. Mail.

Did you ever stop to think how symbolic the average post office building is? The flag is in front and the mail is behind.

The post office uses a phrase that has always fascinated me: UNDE-LIVERABLE AS ADDRESSED. I've heard speeches like that.

It doesn't make sense, like putting RUSH on a letter.

I can understand the postal workers wanting more money. I can understand the postal workers wanting job security. What bothers me is—do they really need Gucci mailbags?

What kind of a name is that for a hurricane—David or Frederick or Gloria? What the Weather Bureau needs is a name that's synony-mous with disaster, destruction, and demolishment. Something like Hurricane Parcel Post.

FRAGILE labels are very important at the post office. If you hear the sound of glass breaking, they tell you what package it came from.

Real faith is sending a gallon of ice cream by parcel post.

If you stop to think about it, all of the problems of the post office could be solved if they just followed the name of a very famous mountain—Rushmore.

POVERTY

Our neighborhood was so poor, kids used to join the Campfire Girls just to get warm!

We were so poor, we used to do all of our shopping at the day-old bakery. I was sixteen before I found out that whole wheat isn't green.

We were so poor, a fad diet was meat.

PRESIDENT

It must be wonderful to be President of the United States, to tune in the Seven O'Clock News and spend the next half hour saying, "I know. I know. I know."

————— has learned a great truth about his job. He's been President for two months and already he's six months behind in his work.

Incidentally, has anyone noticed that sign on the stern of the Ship of State? STUDENT DRIVER?

The way the President is using the media, there could be a new address for the White House: 1600 Madison Avenue.

It's unnerving the way the President keeps asking for support. I think we've elected our first orthopedic President.

Is it true that last week the President came back from Congress and started a brand-new group: Presidents Without Partners?

Being Vice-President of the United States is very time-consuming because you have to repeat everything. For instance, a phone call goes like this: "Hello? This is Vice-President Bush. ——— Bush. ———B-U-S-H."

PRICES

I went into one store where the prices were so high, it's the first time I ever saw a cash register wearing a mask.

Stores really know how to rub it in. Yesterday I saw a price tag with racing stripes.

We finally know what they mean by the "high rent district." It's the area west of the Atlantic and east of the Pacific.

PROPERTY TAXES

You can't really call them property taxes. They're more like a Bermuda Triangle for money.

People really get upset about the property tax. It's the first time I ever saw anybody get tennis elbow from shaking a fist.

I won't say what homeowners are getting, but when you go down to the Property Tax Office they carry you across the threshold.

You don't know how it feels to be writing out a check for $2000 in property taxes while the termites are standing around betting which way it will fall.

PUBLIC RELATIONS

Public relations goes all the way back to the Garden of Eden— when Adam asked for a bigger leaf.

If you're in public relations, you can always tell when you've lost your credibility. On Halloween, people come around and try to tip over your office.

An image problem is when your P.R. is P.U.

Public relations is the fine art of making sure that something is no sooner done than said.

If you don't think P.R. works, consider the millions and millions and millions of Americans who now think yogurt tastes good.

I'm always impressed by a profession that has such an all-encompassing name. It reminds me of the call girl who decided to go straight after five years in the business but she didn't know how to account for the time on her résumé. So she finally put down: 1972 to 1977—Public Relations.

The trouble with being in public relations is you're always on call. You're looking at the only fella in history who was ever operated on for an ingrown beeper.

P.R. is when you never met a man you didn't hype.

RAILROADS

One railroad is trying to drum up passenger business by showing X-rated movies. Maybe you heard about it. It's called the Porny Express.

Then there's the sad story of the railroad executive who was hired by the subway system and it was a total disaster. The first thing he did was eliminate all the passenger trains.

Criticize the railroads all you like but you have to admit the gravy train is always on time.

READING

Have you noticed how kids are turning back to literature? My son spent the whole weekend reading three T-shirts.

The hardest job a modern writer has is communicating with kids. How do you get a T-shirt into a typewriter?

I've mistrusted our local librarian ever since I found *The Hunchback of Notre Dame* in the section marked FOOTBALL.

Everything is relative. I saw a fella reading a copy of *Hustler* hidden inside a copy of *Playboy*.

Why is it that college textbooks always seem to come with 850 pages and two dozen periods?

I just saw a scary thing—a large-print edition of a magazine for hunters.

Don't believe everything you read. Even people who lose at Russian Roulette have wills that say: "Being of sound mind—"

When I first started reading novels, they'd describe a couple as being intimate. In those days, that didn't mean too much to a kid. I always figured they used the same toothbrush.

Reading is drinking from the fountain of knowledge. TV is the diuretic.

REAL ESTATE

"There was an old lady who lived in a shoe." Now that's what I call a real estate salesman!

I love to listen to real estate salesmen. When it comes to houses, you don't have to go to Alaska to get a snow job!

You have to interpret real estate ads. Like "Early American cottage with a certain air about it." That means there's a pig farm next door.

Another favorite phrase is "handyman's delight." That means the only thing that works is you!

No, Virginia, a homing pigeon is not someone who buys real estate by telephone.

There seems to be one basic given in real estate: what God has forsaken, developers haven't.

As I was trying to explain to my teenager today: "Of course Thoreau was happy with Walden Pond. Do you know what waterfront property is going for?"

What amazes me is the way their attitude changes when you're trying to sell instead of buy. I once called in a real estate agent to sell a house and I said, "It has two wings." He said, "Most turkeys do!"

Have you noticed how troubles always seem to come in bunches? This morning I read that the house I sold for $50,000 in 1975 was just resold for $342,000. And two minutes later I had to have something removed from my ear—a gun.

RELIGION

Judgment Day is God's audit.

There's a definite return to religion in this country. A recent poll showed that 62% of all Americans believe in miracles. Half are churchgoers and the rest are Cubs fans.

I've come to this conclusion: the only way I'm going to get to heaven is if there's a typographic error in the Ten Commandments.

Faith is when you can feel, touch, hear, or see something you can't feel, touch, hear, or see.

Sometimes it takes a crisis to get our faith back on track. I've never seen a person pray to Blue Cross.

We're living in a time when faith, prayer, and belief in a greater power is more necessary than ever before. Don't take my word for it. Ask anyone who roots for the (CELLAR TEAM).

Religion has always been a part of politics. For years, voters have looked at some of the candidates and said, "Good Lord!"

The true test of humility is when you can say grace before eating crow.

There's a time and place for everything. For instance, saying: "But enough about me—let's talk about you!" is fine at a cocktail party. In a confession box, not so good.

As Adam and Eve said as they left the Garden of Eden, "Well, so much for Assertiveness Training!"

Some people believe that Noah left the ark on Mount Ararat and five thousand years later it's still there. Which proves three things: the ark did exist; it was very well built; and there is no alternate-side-of-the-street parking on Mount Ararat.

I've often wished that Moses were alive today. He could part the retirement land I bought in Florida.

There have always been those who look for the easy way. As one of the multitude said when Moses came down with the two tablets of stone: "You don't have it in paperback?"

I think our minister is going too far in his attempt to make the Bible understandable to teenagers. For instance, he said that Moses came down from Mount Sinai with the Ten Commandments—on two T-shirts.

THE TEN COMMANDMENTS AREN'T A MULTIPLE CHOICE.

I teach Sunday School and hearing kids pray can be a rather unnerving experience. Last Sunday I heard one kid saying: "Our Father who art in 7-Eleven."

I love that church in San Francisco called Our Lady of Procrastination. They hold services on Tuesday afternoon.

I don't like to watch a church service that's brought to me on TV. When I sing "Nearer, My God, to Thee"—I feel that I should be the one who moves.

Our new minister is really making a big hit with the congregation. As one little old lady put it: "When this minister prays, he asks the Lord for things the other minister didn't even know He had!"

As I try to explain to my wife, I do not sleep through the sermon on Sunday mornings. It's just that we should all make a joyful noise unto the Lord—and mine is zzzzzzzzzz.

I'll never forget our hometown choir—sometimes known as The Off-Keys of the Kingdom.

Last Sunday the new furnace went into operation at our church. We're warm-again Christians!

There's really an ecumenical spirit in the air. It's the first time I ever heard a Salvation Army band playing "Hava Nagila."

There's a new religious movement that was inspired by the stock market—shorn-again Christians.

I was commenting to my neighbor about how many great runners seem to come from theological schools. Why, just last week a seminary student ran the mile in four minutes, ten seconds. My neighbor said, "Lots of people run the mile in four minutes, ten seconds." I said, "On their knees?"

The blizzard of (YEAR) made me grateful for one thing—that the Supreme Court didn't ban praying on highways.

RESTAURANT PRICES

My funds are at a low ebb,
Of cash I am bereft;
It's sad when I read a menu—
It's always from right to left.

Have you ever gone into one of those chic downtown restaurants for lunch? It's like the spot market for food.

I hate to go to a very fine restaurant. There's something about driving home and realizing that every burp has cost you $8.73.

You look at the bill and you don't know if you're eating out or buying in.

You always know you're in trouble when your date gets a menu that doesn't have any prices and you get a menu that looks like the work sheet for the federal budget.

And so you try to subtly influence what she orders by inventing axioms—like, never eat lobster in any month that has a Saturday in it.

But I notice that even the most exclusive restaurants have a Special of the Day. It's their way of allowing you to save face. It's always something exotic—like Day-Old Beef Wellington. . . . Or sometimes they really rub it in—Steak au Poorvre.

Remember when you used to go to Chinese restaurants because they were always so inexpensive? No more. I ordered Moo Goo Gai Pan. It's the first time I was ever charged separately for Moo, Goo, and Gai.

Prices have gone crazy. There's a new Italian restaurant that charges $8.00 for spaghetti, $9.00 for lasagna, and $10 for manicotti. It's called the Golden Starches.

RESTAURANTS

It's amazing how many restaurants make you think of cookouts. You feel like going into the kitchen and saying to the cook, "Out!"

A lot of people are intimidated by the names of Chinese dishes and sometimes it's better just to accept them. One time I asked a waiter what Pork Almond Rice Ding meant. He said, "Well, Pork Almond Rice are what we put in the microwave oven." I said, "And Ding?" He said, "That's the timer."

I had a terrible row in a French restaurant over a food additive. I asked for ketchup.

They just opened a very exclusive restaurant in (RURAL TOWN). You order Gatorade and they ask you what year.

Their specialty is Poulet à la Chevrolet. That's a chicken that was run over by a pickup truck.

I go to one of those little Italian restaurants that cater to young lovers. You can order pizza four different ways: with sausage, pepperoni, mushrooms, or Certs.

Whenever I look at a menu, I can't help but wonder if Stroganoff was a fella who complained a lot.

Messing with a reservation can be a very dangerous thing. Don't take my word for it. Ask Custer.

We had a rather disturbing thing happen last week. The wife of one of our employees tried to poison him. Fortunately, he eats in the company cafeteria—so it didn't take.

We're particularly proud of our company cafeteria. A subsidy keeps the prices down and a Di-Gel keeps the food down.

RETIREMENT

Work is the recreation of the retired.

The nicest part about retirement is when paying the income tax becomes a spectator sport.

Retirees were even mentioned in the Bible. Remember that story about the multitude that loafs and fishes?

Retirement is when your wife realizes she never gave your secretary enough sympathy.

The first few months of retirement are always a difficult period. It's when husbands ask, "What in the world did you do all day while I was at work?" And wives answer, "Better."

As any boss will tell you, workers fall into two categories: those who begin their retirement and those who continue their retirement.

When a good salesman retires, it means different things to different people. To management it means saying good-bye to a talented and loyal associate. To staff it means losing daily contact with a tried and true friend. And to the controller it means 850 unused business cards.

I work for a very cheap outfit. Very cheap. We had one fella retire after fifty-two years of faithful service—and they gave him a testimonial coffee break.

Retirement is when you have this total sense of freedom. You almost feel like picking up the phone, dialing the office, and calling in well.

The nice part about retirement is, it makes it possible for you to do and say all the things you've always wanted to do and say. Last week a public school teacher retired after forty years in the profession—and as she drove away from the school, there was a big sign on the back of the car: KISS MY CLASS!

I keep telling my retired friends not to worry. The Social Security system has as much chance of going bankrupt as Mexico.

If you're retired and you hear about Social Security going broke, don't worry. If you're retired and you read about Social Security paying out $5 billion a year more than it's taking in, don't worry. But if you're retired and you notice your Social Security check is postdated—worry.

The problem with retiring on a fixed income: it starts off with a farewell dinner—then, in a few years, a farewell to lunch—then a farewell to breakfast.

Retirement is when you go from spending six hours a week in your garden for the exercise to spending thirty hours a week in your garden for the food.

Retirement is when the only thing you sink your teeth into is a glass.

I never really believed retired people were eating dog food until that poll came out. The one that lists their four favorite forms of recreation: golf, television, shuffleboard, and chasing cars.

There's a reason why so many retirement communities start off the day by singing, "Oh, say, can you see by the dawn's early light?" Who can afford glasses?

Retirement poses many challenges. For instance, it's very unsettling when you sell the house you've lived in all of your life and move into a high-rise. How do you mow a lobby?

I want only three things when I retire: a good pension, a paid-up mortgage, and a rocking chair with cruise control.

Retirement is when Memory Lane becomes an Interstate.

Retirement is when your wife gives you a vitamin E inhalator—because sex is mostly in your head.

Retirement is when you've come a long way, baby—and you're just about out of gas.

Retirement is when you're still filled with the vital juices of life, only now they're prune.

Our local bar has a retirement martini. Instead of an olive, it has a prune.

I always like going to retirement parties because they're different. Where else can you get Geritol on draft?

Inflation is like this. Two years ago, if you retired, they gave you a gold watch. Last year, if you retired, they gave you a silver watch. Now, if you retire, they give you ten cents and a number to dial for the time.

RETIREMENT ROASTS

I want to tell you something about the man we honor tonight. When he first announced his retirement, fifty people stood outside his office with tears in their eyes—waiting to ask for his parking space.

Throughout his thirty years with this company, ————— has earned a well-deserved reputation for his "can do" spirit. Whenever there was something to do, he was in the can.

I won't say how many mistakes he's made during his thirty-five years with our company but as a token of our esteem and admiration—(FIRST NAME), we had your eraser bronzed.

ROASTS

I know this is supposed to be a roast, but I'm a firm believer in only saying something good about a person—and, boy, is this good!

He is a man who is known for his unfailing good humor—which, in turn, he owes to three things: an understanding wife, a loving family, and industrial-strength Ripple.

Dull? One time he was drowning and his entire life passed before him. Halfway through he got up and left.

Lazy? If money grew on trees, he'd stand around with a rake waiting for autumn.

Cheap? Yesterday he tried to margarine me up!

Cheap? When he breaks a dollar bill, he sings "Auld Lang Syne."

You might say he has financial arthritis. Every time he reaches for a check—he winces.

Cheap? Who else do you know goes to a massage parlor on standby?

Old? He's reached the age where he has to look at *Playboy* through an interpretor.

He's a man of letters—N.G.

He had an embarrassing experience with a spiritualist medium last week. She said, "Think of me as an instrument of communication —your telephone to talk to the other world." And that's what caused the problem. His phone is a Touch-Tone.

Shy? I happen to know that he once failed a lie detector test. He never got past, "In my humble opinion . . ."

CONCLUDING A ROAST: And so we come to this happy ending. The audience is glad because it's happy—and I think (ROASTEE) is glad because it's ending.

ROASTS (RESPONDING TO)

As I came here tonight, I realized that this would be an evening pregnant with the potential for oratorical brilliance. Unfortunately, none of the preceding speakers has proven to be the father.

If you recall, we began this evening with an invocation and we thanked the Lord for what we were about to receive. Considering what I received, I think the Lord may have overdone it.

I've always said that all I want out of life is a little appreciation—and that's about as little appreciation as I could imagine.

First, let me congratulate the previous speaker for his courage in approaching such a vast subject with such a half-vast speech.

Needless to say, this has been an evening to remember. I say an evening to remember because I want to get it right when I talk to my lawyer in the morning.

Sitting here this last hour, I got the distinct impression we should have heard the minutes of the previous meeting and dispensed with the reading of those speeches.

First, let me thank the Program Chairman, the Program Committee, and everybody else responsible for this wonderful evening—not to mention the previous speakers. And considering what they said about me, I don't think I will mention the previous speakers.

It is a great pleasure to be here tonight. I can't remember when I've been with a group that has conveyed to me so many human rights—and lefts—and rabbit punches—and karate chops.

RESPONSE WHEN YOU'RE ROASTED AT A DINNER: I've listened with great interest to all that has been said about me tonight and, in response, I want to thank the Program Committee for what can only be described as a religious experience. Like the good Lord, you have prepared a table before me in the presence of mine enemies.

ROLLER SKATING

The world land speed record of 622 miles an hour was broken today—by a roller skater in San Francisco. . . . His name has been withheld pending notification of the next of kin.

Roller skating is when you're moved along by a lot of little wheels. It's like the bureaucracy.

Everyone is roller skating. Last night two hookers were arrested for street rolling.

The first lesson you learn when going roller skating is that there is no longer such a thing as a cheap skate.

Have you priced roller skates? Expensive? It's cheaper to strap on two Volkswagens!

Nowadays, the wheels on roller skates are made of a specially treated, scientifically compounded polyurethane. In my day, we would have settled for their just being round.

When I was a kid, when you went roller skating, you just assumed you were going to get hurt. That's right. Mothers used to buy doormats that didn't show the blood.

A real good day was when you came home and you still had thirty-two teeth—twenty-nine in your mouth and three in your pocket.

But roller skating has changed a lot from when I was a kid. Now you wear knee pads, elbow pads, shin guards, and a helmet. I didn't have that much protection on D-Day.

There must be a divine order to life. How else would you explain the fact that, just when hospitals have so many unused beds— adults took up roller skating?

Roller skating is the sport that allows you to stand absolutely still while hurtling toward disaster. It's a little like Congress.

There's only one problem if you're middle-aged and you get killed roller skating. If your will says, "Being of sound mind"—it can be challenged.

RUNNING

Running is a very old sport. Some people think it began with a messenger in Greece. Others think it began with a tourist in Mexico.

Actually, fellas running down the street in their shorts is nothing new. It's just that the starting line used to be a closet.

The statistics tell the story. They show that every year there are a few million more runners—while the birth rate is declining. Which can mean only one thing: for the first time in history, there are more Americans interested in running than in catching.

Show me a woman who answers the phone and hears nothing but heavy breathing—and I'll show you a woman whose husband has taken up running.

The problem of middle-aged runners can be summed up by this exchange during a recent marathon. One said, "I don't want to brag, but I've got the body of a twenty-year-old." And the other said, "Give it back. You're getting it all wrinkled."

There's even a name for middle-aged runners—the Gray Panters.

If you're a runner, the Boston Marathon is like playing the Palace. They say that last week almost 5000 people ran in Boston. I know. I've lived in neighborhoods like that myself.

There are two critical points every marathon runner has to cope with: the sixteen-mile point, where you're afraid you're going to die; and the twenty-two mile point, where you're afraid you won't.

And running is great if you're overweight. You don't lose any pounds but if you run ten miles on a hot day people stand so far away you *look* thin.

It's only a question of time before somebody writes a sequel to *The Complete Book of Running*. It'll be called *The Complete Book of Aching*.

There are now so many people running ten miles a day, it could be a problem. There might not be enough heart attacks to go around.

Runners are perfectionists. They won't do anything unless they have the right equipment. I know a runner who dropped dead. It's the first time I ever saw an Adidas coffin.

And runners develop terrific stamina. At the funeral there were six pallbearers. Five were friends and one was him.

Running has revolutionized our way of life. Thanks to running, millions of Americans are dropping three things: pounds, inhibitions, and dead.

I don't want to shake anybody up, but running can be dangerous. Look what happened to (LOSING CANDIDATE).

Running is when you use every muscle in your body. Incidentally, there are no muscles in the brain.

Running ten miles a day isn't as simple as it looks. Your feet have to control your stride; your feet have to control your balance; your feet have to control your thrust. One might even go so far as to say, if you run ten miles a day, you've gotta have your brains in your feet!

I have only one thing to say about runners: anyone who says they run ten miles a day with their muscles aching, their hearts pounding, and their lungs on fire, because it makes them feel good—will lie about other things as well.

RUSSIA

I think Russia is carrying excess to excess.

I don't mind exchanging ballet companies with the Russians. I don't mind exchanging art exhibitions with the Russians. I don't even mind exchanging technology with the Russians. But when we start exchanging weather with the Russians, that's going too far!

I'm not going to worry just as long as Russia stays ahead of us in one thing—dissidents.

A couple recently returned from a sightseeing trip to the U.S.S.R. and related a conversation they had with the Russian student assigned to show them Moscow. They asked the student what she would most like to be after her stint as an American tourist guide. Without hesitation she answered, "An American tourist."

Modern merchandising hasn't quite made it to Russia. You can tell that by the signs in department stores saying: IF YOU DON'T SEE WHAT YOU WANT—WANT WHAT YOU SEE!

The Russians have really perfected long-range agriculture. Every year they plant millions of acres of wheat in Russia—and every year they harvest it in Kansas.

All of Europe measures things by the metric system but I'm still suspicious of it. Look at how Russia is trying to meet us halfway.

Anybody who says the Russians are looking for a fifty-fifty agreement on nuclear arms either doesn't understand fractions—or Russians.

If we really want to stop the Russians in Europe, it's easy. We take NATO out and put the (WINNING FOOTBALL TEAM) in.

Russia is the originator of the Teflon Treaty. Nothing sticks.

I don't want to put down the Russians, but with some countries an agreement lasts for decades. With other countries an agreement lasts for years. With the Russians, you use an egg timer.

Thanks to Russia, we finally know the true meaning of détente. It stands for:

> Skip the bother and skip the fuss—
> You play by rules but don't ask us!

Maybe it's time we took a more realistic view of the world. Russians think nothing of crossing another country's border. We stop if a card says DO NOT PASS GO.

The Russians have now grabbed so much land, they get fan letters from developers.

If all the Russians really want is access to warm water, there's no problem. I could let them have our kiddie pool—and three kiddies.

I'll say one thing for our allies: they operate on the Buddy System. When it comes to taking a stand against Russia, they say, "Not me, Buddy!"

SALAD BARS

This is the time of year when things slowly change from green to yellow to brown. In New England, they're called "leaves." In California, they're called "salad bars."

A salad bar is where people go to exchange germs.

I go to one of those Detroit salad bars. Every six months they change the oil.

I just don't have an instinct for business. I once opened a day-old salad bar.

SALESMEN

Did you ever get the feeling your Sales Department couldn't sell aspirin on Wall Street?

Every time I see our competitor in his brand-new Rolls-Royce, I get very philosophical. I say: "There but for the grace of our Sales Department go I!"

This year we really mean business. We've just coated all of the salesmen's desk chairs with Teflon.

Salesmen really understand the need for prayer. They're used to staying in touch with the home office.

Every morning the boss holds an inspirational sales meeting. First he says a prayer for all those salesmen who have passed beyond— their quotas.

Is this man a salesman? He could sell NO SMOKING signs in Winston-Salem.

Is this man a salesman? He sells carbon paper to Xerox!

Is this man a salesman? During World War II he sold pension plans to kamikaze pilots!

Is this man a salesman? He could sell leaves to a homeowner.

Is this man a salesman? Last Christmas he convinced his wife that polyester is the generic name for mink.

I couldn't help but overhear our neighbor bragging to a friend about her husband. She said he's such a dedicated salesman, he even subscribes to a magazine just to learn how to be more dynamic, more aggressive, and more of a go-getter. She's never looked at the magazine but she can tell by the title. Her friend said, "What's the title?" She said, *"Hustler!"*

My wife has an interesting way of looking at things. She thinks that, deep down, every man is a traveling salesman.

SCHOOLS

It's incredible the way kids react to their first day in school. I spent the whole morning trying to convince my five-year-old there was no such thing as a Killer Kindergarten.

Schoolteachers go on strike for the same reason that lion tamers smoke a cigarette before going into the cage. If you knew what was coming, would *you* hurry?

I can remember when I was a kid we used to write the answers to questions on our fingernails. One time I got so nervous, I chewed up two years of Intermediate Algebra!

I went to a very hip school. Very hip. We had the world's only bugle and finger-snapping corps.

And it was a very macho school. It's the first time I ever saw a debating team take steroids.

SCIENCE FICTION

Some people are confused as to the difference between science fiction and fantasy, but they shouldn't be. Science fiction is a vehicle that travels at the speed of light and is operated by an advanced civilization. Fantasy is a vehicle that travels at the speed of light and is operated by the post office.

This morning I had an out-of-body experience. My mind said to my body, "Today we're going to run ten miles, do 200 push-ups and swim 300 laps in the pool." And my body said, "Out!"

After all these years, I'm still impressed by the starship *Enterprise*. For those of you who have never seen the starship *Enterprise*, picture a Piper Cub that was built on a government contract.

I like science fiction, but I really think they should add a touch of realism to it. For instance, when Captain Kirk says: "Activate the cyclotronic sensors into 3XZero sequence with an intermodal time warp!" Just once, couldn't somebody say, "Huh?"

Have you noticed how science fiction movies are now based on much more realistic themes? For instance, that new one—*The Pothole That Swallowed Chicago!*

One science fiction movie is set in a police station. It had to be set in a police station. They finally found out what Gordon was flashing.

Now they're working on a science fiction movie that's going to be a tremendous hit in every big city in America. It's all about this giant hubcap that steals vandals!

It's a fantastic movie. All about human beings who encounter an alien presence. It's a little like asking the boss for a raise.

SENATE

You have to grant that the Senate chaplain has a sense of humor—particularly when he looks out over the assembled group and says, "Forgive them, Father, for they know not what they do!"

The Senate has a $135-million office building. It's named after a famous leader who is no longer with us—Louis XIV.

I won't say how the politicians justify this building but it's the first time I ever saw a senator vote with a stocking over his head.

Actually there are very few luxuries in the new Senate Office Building. Take away the cashmere roller towels and it's almost spartan.

As I understand it, the biggest expense is the elevators. Six of them go to the top floor, three of them go to the basement, and one of them goes to Brazil.

Unfortunately, taxpayers are always asking dumb questions like, "How can you spend $135 million on one building?" The politicians answer, "Easy. Just look at the goldprints. Every washroom has hot and cold running water." The taxpayers say, "Lots of washrooms have hot and cold running water." And the politicians say, "Perrier?"

SEX

We call them the "good old days" because we weren't good; we weren't old; and we were talking about the nights.

I respond to most appeals but my favorite charity is still the Sex Drive.

I can't understand why lovemaking is always referred to in theatrical terms. For instance, why do they have to call it your sexual performance? Personally, I have no problems with performance. With me, it's the encores.

I must be oversexed. I look at a girl on the street and I can't help but think that under her coat, her sweater, her dress, her slip, and her panty hose—that girl is stark naked!

I'm so naive I thought kinky sex is when the girl wears curlers.

I'm so naive, I thought kinky sex was a wrinkled *Playboy*.

I had an embarrassing thing happen to me last week. I answered one of those very personal classified ads in an underground newspaper. It said: "Voluptuous liberated temptress desires to meet handsome, uninhibited male to share interest in S-M." 1. I'm not handsome. 2. I'm not uninhibited. And 3. I thought S-M meant Steve Martin.

Happiness is doing 55 per hour—at an orgy.

They say sex can cause a temporary loss of memory. Now, where was I?

I overheard a fascinating conversation at a party last night. A fella went up to a girl and said, "How about us going off in a corner and doing a little cuddling?" She said, "That'll be the day." He said, "Then how about us going up to my apartment and doing a little loving?" She said, "That'll be the day." He said, "Well, how about us taking my private jet and spending the weekend at my château in France?" She said, "This'll be the day!"

It's very easy to tell a compatible couple at a winter resort. He holds his hands toward the fire and she turns her back to the fire.

My uncle fooled around. I mean, he really fooled around. When they buried him, he had the only grave with a back door.

I just figured out what happened to all those fellas who used to go to burlesque shows for the comics. They now read *Playboy* for the politicians.

Have you seen that new bumper sticker: RABBITS DIE FOR YOUR SINS?

You know you've broached the subject too early when your kids want to color the pictures in the sex manual.

You never hear about sex in Ireland. The best-selling book over there is *The Joy of Nix.*

SHOW BUSINESS

A performer has to judge, to analyze, to assess every audience. For instance, if you see the first few rows drinking beer through a straw—out goes the Marcel Proust bit.

Believe it or not, the "Tonight Show" was responsible for an argument on my honeymoon. It was the first night. My wife was getting undressed and she caught me peeking—at Johnny Carson.

Lying in bed is the traditional way to watch Johnny Carson. I once saw him in person and didn't recognize him without my toes.

I know a professional comedian who went back to selling houses because it's so much easier. To get a laugh, all you have to do is give the price.

Please don't sit too close. Some people are known to have actually been scorched by my talent.

Fame is a happy condition of uncertain duration—like spending your wedding night in a hammock.

Any radio station that pulls 5000 watts should speak louder.

CONTEST: Welcome to our ————— annual ————————— contest—where the elite meet to compete.

You don't know what fear is until you drop your contact lens during a tap-dancing class.

SMOKING

Winston Churchill was never seen without his cigar. If smoking is hazardous to health, in this case it was Hitler's.

My wife is really against smoking. Yesterday she spent three hours trying to convince a fella to stop smoking. She said, "Just look at the tips of your fingers. They're yellow." He said, "I know. I'm Chinese!"

I'm pretty upset about this antismoking campaign. I'm ready to fight anybody who's trying to take away my gusto—or my coughing fits.

It's very hard to give up a habit. You know how some people are chain smokers? I'm a chain quitter.

I know that "life is a cabaret." I just don't want anybody firing the cigarette girl.

My wife says it's very helpful to be married to a pipe smoker. Whenever I go out of town and she gets lonely for me, she just stands in back of a bus and inhales.

We're living in a crazy mixed-up world. In some states it's against the law to smoke in an elevator—but the Muzak can still play "Smoke Gets in Your Eyes."

I have only had one ambition in life: to go to the annual meeting of the American Tobacco Company and ask to sit in the no-smoking section.

SNOW

I'm praying for spring. I just can't take snow for an answer.

I don't want to find fault, but I wonder if God ever considered having snow fall *up?*

After what happened this month, I'm convinced that what the world really needs is a power shovel.

How come snowbanks are never overdrawn?

I haven't seen this much white since I ran out of Grecian Formula!

> Snow is so light and so bright and so fluffy,
> Unless you must shovel it—then it's a toughy!

This is the time of year when you get that same dumb advice—that if you're middle-aged you shouldn't shovel wet snow. What they never tell you is how to make it dry. You ever try to give Dristan to a snowbank?

One thing has always amazed me about snowstorms. When it comes time to shovel it, I can never understand how three kids can disappear in a five-room house.

Once upon a time a father read that a middle-aged man should not shovel wet snow because he could have a heart attack. So he called in his teenager and said, "Son, a middle-aged man should not shovel wet snow because he could have a heart attack. So would you do it for me?" The son said yes. And the father had a heart attack.

Snow is the great leveler. No matter how expensive a neighborhood you live in, it's Skid Row.

I have no objection to snow falling. What I object to is *me* falling.

It's very interesting the way City Hall has handled the snow removal problem. So far there are a lot more open mouths than streets.

Now you know why the capital of the United States isn't (SNOW-BOUND CITY). I mean, how would that sound—the President leaving the White House on Flexible Flyer One?

What can you really say about (SNOWBOUND CITY)? It's a nice place to visit but I wouldn't want to shovel there.

"Where are the snows of yesteryear?" If you live in (SNOWBOUND CITY)—right outside!

The biggest problem in (SNOWBOUND CITY) is getting used to calling your attic window the front door.

New York is doing its best to get back to business as usual. The city is shoveling out Times Square and the muggers are shoveling out Central Park.

SOCIAL SECURITY

Have you seen what Social Security is taking out this year? Why is it that the tax bite never needs Poli-Grip?

If you consider what we pay in and what we can expect to get back, what can you really say about Social Security? We've got the bread and they've got the crust.

People have mixed feelings about paying into Social Security. It's a little like the Scotsman who put a $20 bill into the church collection plate by mistake—and as he watched it disappear down the aisle, said: "Ah, well, 'tis gone to heaven—so to hell with it!"

The President has a sign on his desk: THE BUCK STOPS HERE. I just hope they don't put up that same sign at Social Security.

They just put mistletoe up over the entrance to the Social Security Administration, which is very appropriate. It's for people who want to kiss their money good-bye.

Have you read what the government is going to take out of your paycheck for Social Security? I think they finally nationalized mugging.

For those of you who aren't familiar with Social Security deductions, they're like a vacuum cleaner for money.

Taxation is now based on the same principles as that razor with two blades. The income tax takes most of what you have and Social Security takes what's left.

The motto of charity is GIVE TILL IT HURTS. The motto of Social Security is HURT TILL IT GIVES.

I really worry about the soundness of Social Security. What if I reach sixty-five and there isn't enough poverty to go around?

Children are a comfort to you in your old age—but, like Social Security, it's nowhere near as much as you had expected.

The government has a fantastic sense of P.R. The latest plan is midget letter carriers to make your Social Security checks look bigger.

SPEAKERS' AD-LIBS

It is a little intimidating to be here tonight. As I look around at this head table, I'm the only one up here I haven't heard of.

I'm sorry I'm late. I followed a used car dealer at confession. Had to wait four hours and fifteen minutes.

AFTER A BIG LAUGH: I haven't heard a laugh like that since I asked about a 6% mortgage.

AFTER A MODEST SPEAKER: Our speaker failed to mention that he also (LIST FURTHER ACCOMPLISHMENTS). When it comes to blowing his own horn, a Gabriel he ain't!

AFTER A VERBAL MISTAKE: There will now be a short pause while I open my mouth and change feet.

AFTER A TOO LONG SPEECH: I want to thank —————— for that marvelously laid back speech. What it laid back is our schedule by thirty-five minutes.

I know he had a message for posterity but I didn't expect it to be hand-delivered.

I knew we were in trouble when I saw my calendar watch change during the soup course.

BLOW ON THE MICROPHONE TO SEE IF IT IS ON. PAUSE. BLOW ON IT AGAIN. PAUSE. BLOW ON IT A THIRD TIME. EXPLAIN: If there's one thing I hate, it's a dusty microphone.

IF A LARGE BANNER OR SIGN IS VISIBLE: I love that decoration. Looks like a name tag for Orson Welles.

IF YOU ARE SHORT AND HAVE TO LOWER THE MICROPHONE: I can rise to any occasion but not to any microphone.

IF YOU'RE GIVING A SLIDE PRESENTATION AND ONE OF THEM IS MISSING, LOOK AT THE BLANK SCREEN AND COMMENT: I love this picture. Looks like the results of (PERSONALITY)'s aptitude test.

IF YOU YAWN: I'm sorry. I was just thinking about the new TV season.

INTERRUPTION: Sir, I hate to argue with someone who's mis-informed—and for a very good reason. I'm always afraid they might be doing the same thing.

TO A HOSTILE QUESTIONER GIVING A SPEECH RATHER THAN A QUESTION DURING THE Q. & A. PERIOD: Sir, would you please ask your question? Time is running on and your mouth is running off.

I haven't heard anything like this since I said hello to Howard Cosell.

UNUSUAL OUTFIT: That's what I call a class action suit. It has a lot more action than class.

WHEN A JOKE DIES: Did you ever get the feeling your talent is on HOLD?

WHEN RECEIVING AN HONOR: Thank you very much for this valued award. I want you all to know that you have given me 100% of the daily adult requirement of happiness.

WHEN SOMEONE SAYS OR DOES SOMETHING INAPPROPRIATE: I'm just glad I'm wearing this watch. It's shockproof.

WHEN SOMETHING GOES WRONG: Darn! Darn—that's the generic term for (MOUTH SOME CURSE WORDS).

WHEN THE AUDIENCE ANTICIPATES A PUNCHLINE: I think you people are listening faster than I'm talking.

WHEN THE LIGHTS GO OUT: It's all right. We have just temporarily lost our picture.

Hello, electric company? The check is in the mail.

I'm just glad this happened now. It usually happens three seconds after I've said something like: "And if I'm lying, may I be struck blind on this very spot!"

WHEN THE MEETING ROOM IS TOO COLD: Before we go any further, I want you to know that we have contacted the hotel manager and asked him to send someone up to take a look at the air conditioning. If it's in the next fifteen minutes, we asked for an air conditioning maintenance man. If it isn't in the next fifteen minutes, we asked for Admiral Byrd.

First I want to pay tribute to the person who runs the air conditioning in this hotel—sometimes known as Nanook of the Thermostat. . . . I never thought I'd get to experience July in Washington and February in Alaska, at the same time.

WHEN THE MEETING ROOM IS TOO HOT: And now, for my encore, I'm going to fry an egg on the air conditioner.

What say we all just adjourn, go to Safeway, and feel cold melons?

WHEN THE MICROPHONE DOESN'T WORK: Wouldn't it be great if we could get one of these for Howard Cosell?

This happens to be an extremely valuable piece of equipment. Do you realize what Richard Nixon would have paid for a microphone that didn't work?

WHEN THE MICROPHONE DOESN'T WORK: I didn't know (YOUR COMPETITION) made sound systems.

WHEN THE MICROPHONE COMES ON AGAIN: Is it working? Oh, good! (THEN MIME THE RESUMPTION OF YOUR SPEECH BUT WITHOUT ANY SOUND.)

WHEN THE MICROPHONE KEEPS DROPPING DOWN: Does anybody have any vitamin E?

WHEN THE PREVIOUS SPEAKER HAS GONE VERY WELL: They say that life is unfair—but I never realized how unfair until I was asked to follow ——————.

WHEN THINGS ARE GOING BADLY: I feel like I'm in the Goodyear blimp and I just saw a woodpecker!

WHEN THINGS ARE GOING DOWNHILL: We're pioneering a new concept in programs tonight—participatory failure!

WHEN YOU ARE LAST ON A VERY LONG PROGRAM: This has really been an incredible evening. They say that the first shall be last and the last shall be first. And so, let me say first, this is the last time I'm not going to go on first.

WHEN YOU FILL IN: The Program Chairman has asked me to come up here and talk on a stopgap basis. He said the minute I see one of you gap—stop!

WHEN YOU GARBLE A SENTENCE: I'm sorry. My mind wandered and my tongue followed it.

We will now pause while the C.I.A. decodes that last sentence.

WHEN YOU GARBLE A SENTENCE, PRECEDE REPEATING IT WITH: And now, let's see that again in slow motion.

WHEN YOU GARBLE WORDING: Let me repeat that. (THEN YOU GARBLE THE WORDING AGAIN.)

And now, I'd like to repeat that in the original English.

For those of you who don't have your Captain Marvel secret decoder ring, let me translate that.

I'm sorry. That's not the speech. I was reading the alphabet soup.

WHEN YOU INTRODUCE SOMEONE BY USING THE WRONG NAME: Now I know what they mean by an identity crisis.

WHEN YOU MAKE A MISTAKE: I think the butterflies in my stomach have just reached my head.

I'd open my mouth to apologize only I'm afraid a foot would fall out.

WHEN YOU PUT YOUR WATCH ON THE LECTERN: I don't want to upset the Program Committee, but this isn't a watch. It's a meter.

WHEN YOU'VE SAID SOMETHING EMBARRASSING: Wouldn't it be great if speeches came with erasers?

WHEN YOU SUBSTITUTE FOR ANOTHER SPEAKER: I want to thank you for that warm and generous applause because it's never easy to be a substitute speaker. The audience always looks on you the same way they look on making out their income tax. They hope for the best but they're prepared for the worst.

SPEAKERS' FEES

As any Program Chairman will tell you, any speaker whose credits beggar description usually has a fee that beggars your treasury.

I've learned one thing as a speaker. When you bring up the subject of a fee and the organization says it's willing to talk turkey—it means your lunch is free.

I'm always a little suspicious of any group that pays a caterer $15 a setting to fill their stomachs—and a speaker five cents a word to fill their minds.

This may sound immodest, but I have to agree with the Program Chairman that, when it comes to speakers, I'm one of the best. Mostly because, to a Program Chairman, the best things in life are free.

SPEECHES

A sinking feeling is what you get in the pit of your stomach when you reach into your pocket for the envelope that contains your speech—and find the envelope that contains your 1040.

A good speech and a calliope have this in common: it's hot air put to a good purpose.

The problem with most televised speeches is, they're presented in living duller.

I always thought a Pap test was trying out your speech on your wife.

The trouble with practicing your speech in front of a mirror—there's always such a dubious look on the face of your audience.

Bullpen: what some people use to write speeches.

A speech text is when you're given artificial recitation.

> This advice to occasional speakers
> I offer and then you can weigh it:
> When you start off with "needless to say"—
> You really don't then have to say it.

The most important thing to remember in giving a speech is to use short, simple words in contiguous juxtaposition.

ORAL SURGERY: cutting your speech in half.

Speeches are like lawns. It's best to keep them short.

Public speaking is a little like taking a vacation. It helps to know the right place to stop.

> A toast to our honored speaker
> And to the speech he brought.
> It was witty, profound, and challenging,
> But, best of all, it was short!

"In conclusion"—I love that phrase. It's like a wake-up call for audiences.

I always know when I'm coming to the end of my speech. It's when the butterflies in my stomach return their seats to a full upright position.

SPORTS

As anyone who saw (LOSING TEAM) play this weekend already knows—not all of the turkeys are waiting for Thanksgiving.

After six months of watching baseball on television, four months of watching football on television, and two months of watching basketball on television—it finally happened. They had to remove something from my bottom—an ingrown sofa.

This morning I woke up so groggy, I started reading the paper upside down. What called it to my attention—(CELLAR TEAM) was leading its division.

Let us never lose sight of that wise old saying, If you can walk ten feet tall through the challenges of life, you will never walk alone. There will always be a basketball coach following you.

Our local college voted to let its athletic director go. It was all because of that six-foot-eleven player he recruited for the team. The chess team.

Last night I went to a hockey game and it was the first time in my life I ever saw a hat trick. How that pigeon got in there I'll never know.

Karate is like proposing marriage. It's so dangerous, you don't use it if you're bluffing!

One of the fastest-growing sports these days is skydiving. You jump out of a plane at 10,000 feet and you head for a little black dot on the ground. And if you don't pull the rip cord in time, it's you!

All you have to do to jump out of an airplane at 10,000 feet is three things—check your parachute, check your rip cord, and check your brains!

I'm not much of a swimmer because I've always been afraid of the water. I take a shower and my entire life passes before my eyes.

I only know one stroke. If I get in over my head, I have one.

One of the fastest-growing sports in America is white-water rafting. For those of you who aren't familiar with white-water rafting —it's what you do when you're mad at your life insurance agent.

It's kinda hard to describe white-water rafting. It's like going over Niagara Falls in a kiddie pool.

This yacht is so big, the life preservers sleep six.

The American lumber industry owes a great deal to winter sports. Its product is used for chalets, skis, splints, and crutches.

The bravest person I know is a skier who's allergic to casts.

Now I know why so few skiers ever kick the habit. Who can kick in a cast?

I've always been fascinated by bobsledding. Do you realize, if it wasn't for that sled, those four people would be arrested?

I just wrote a letter to the Olympic Committee and told them that if the torch ever goes out—the eternal flame—not to worry. They can always come over to our kitchen to relight it. We have the eternal grease fire.

The Russians are very proud of their athletes. The Russian Olympic team is where men are men—and so are women.

STOCKBROKERS

Years ago I was a stockbroker and that's a fascinating business to be in. You'd be surprised how many people used to drive to our office in a Mercedes to get financial advice from people who came to work in a bus.

I don't think my heart can take much more of this. Yesterday my broker called and said, "It's down another five." I said, "What's down another five?" He said, "The thermostat. It's freezing in here!"

Never, never deal with a broker who has a sense of humor. Yesterday I called him up and got a recorded announcement. All it said was: "It's ten o'clock. Do you know where your profits are?"

I always enjoy going up to see my broker because he's ready for anything. At one end of his office there's a square device with a sign saying: IN CASE OF EMERGENCY, BREAK GLASS. It's a window.

They say more accidents occur in the home than anywhere else. That's right. That's where I call my broker from.

I'm getting a little worried about my broker. He just moved into a brand-new three-room ledge.

I like the spirit of the Wall Street broker with the little sign on the door: UP SPOKEN HERE.

Frankly, I've had to stop accepting calls from my broker. I kept getting obscene prices.

STOCK MARKET

I'd like to say a few words about what's happened to the stock market, but I have something in my mouth—my heart.

If you're an incurable optimist, the stock market is penicillin.

My aunt has an incredible memory. Last week she looked up from the paper and said, "It's been fifty-five years since the great crash." She has never forgiven my uncle for dropping that vase.

> They say that it can never happen again,
> The '29 crash we're all mourning.
> So tell me why is it that sometimes I hear
> What sounds like a two-minute warning?

Sometimes I get the feeling it isn't a coincidence that we're celebrating the fifty-fifth anniversary of the Great Crash in buildings with windows that don't open.

An elephant never forgets. I can prove an elephant never forgets. Name me one elephant who's in the stock market!

This is the kind of stock market that only a taxidermist could love. Whether you're a bull or a bear, you wind up getting skinned.

I don't think there was a stock market in Noah's time. The ark only had two pigeons.

The stock market is one of the great educational institutions of our time. It teaches patience, thrift, restraint, how to cope with frustration and all the other things you wouldn't have to know if you weren't in the stock market.

They say the institutions are getting back into the market. What bothers me is, Bellevue is an institution.

In times like these, the stock market is like squeezing a tube of toothpaste in the middle. Half is trying to get out and the other half is getting in deeper.

The way the stock market has been going up and down, up and down, up and down, has really interested a lot of people. Graduates want to make it a career, investors want to make it a hobby, and Disney wants to make it a ride.

There's nothing wrong with the stock market that couldn't be cured by Valium-flavored fingernails.

A visit to the New York Stock Exchange is an experience not to be missed—a tour de loss!

I don't want to seem bitter, but last week my broker called and said, "The Dow Jones broke 1300!" I said, "I know. I'm one of them."

The stock market had another one of its soft-drink days: 7 up, 1400 down.

Playing the stock market is a little like taking the pins out of a new shirt. No matter how careful you are—you still get stuck.

Remember when we only took a bath on Saturday night? Now, thanks to the stock market, we can do it all week long.

Remember when people used to go for broke? Now the stock market brings it to you.

What the stock market really needs is exercise—push-ups!

This is definitely a two-tier market. You shed the first tear when you read what the Dow Jones Average has done and the second tear when you read what your own stocks have done.

Can you imagine explaining to a caveman fighting off a saber-toothed tiger with a spear—why your adrenalin is running because the Dow Jones Average is down twelve points?

There's a brand-new product for anyone who's in the stock market these days—Industrial-Strength Pampers!

I won't say what's been happening in the stock market but one Wall Street bar is serving industrial-strength martinis.

Nowadays you only need three things to be successful in the stock market: money, intelligence, and industrial-strength prayer.

First, let us bow our heads in memory of all those paper profits that have passed away.

I've reached that point with the stock market where this morning I just picked up the phone and said a four-letter word to my broker: "SELL!"

There's a reason why investors feel more confident buying at the peak of a market than at the bottom of a market. It's called the Nerd Instinct.

I'm really glad the stock market has gone up. For a while there, Wall Street was thinking of putting up its own memorial—the Tomb of the Unknown Profit.

I'll never forget how quickly the market turned around. It's the first time I ever saw a broker jump out of a window and make a U-turn.

A stock market rally is when people who have lost their shirt get back a sleeve.

One day the Dow went up so fast, if a stock gained a point they listed it with the losers.

I won't say that speculation is coming back into the stock market, but this morning a fella called his broker and said, "Buy 10,000 shares!" The broker said, "Of what?" He said, "Surprise me."

I owe all of my success in the stock market to one simple action. Many years ago I took up Transcendental Meditation—and the mantra they gave me was "I.B.M."

STOCKS

I had a rather disturbing thing happen last month. I was reading the annual report of a company I own stock in and one of the items was: CASH FLEW—$300,000. So I wrote to the Chairman of the Board and said, "That's CASH FLOW. Your accountant is in error." He wrote back and said, "No, that's CASH FLEW. Our accountant is in Brazil."

Do you ever get the feeling that, in the middle of the night, Count Dracula comes in and bites your stocks on the neck?

A lot of stock is bought on the greater fool theory. You buy a stock and then you look for a greater fool to take it off your hands. A lot of divorces are based on the same theory.

I have always concentrated on one-decision stocks: you buy them, you hold them for many years, and then the only decision you have to make is when to sell them to take the tax loss.

A bull market is when one of your stocks hits 100. A bear market is when five of your stocks hit 100—40, 30, 20, 10, and, "What do you mean, there's no bid?"

Remember that song, "How Deep Is the Ocean, How High Is the Sky?" I think of it every time I look at the price of my stocks and the stacks of my bills.

I have only one thing to say about my stocks: "How low can you get?"

They say that foreign steel is selling for less than it costs. I think they got the idea from my stocks.

I'll say one thing for owning gambling stocks: you may not make any money but it's great for curing hiccups.

When it comes to redundancy, you just can't beat "gambling stocks."

Today we have come together to discuss one of the great philosophical concepts of our time: if a stock falls on Wall Street and nobody sees it—did it really fall?

STUDENTS

Personally, I don't trust all those student demonstrations you see in other countries. Any group of students who get together and claim there is something more important than sex will lie about other things as well.

I watched one of those student demonstrations on TV last night and all I can say is—if they were students, kindergarten must start at thirty-two.

All these students seem to do is demonstrate—they never study. When they wind up with a degree that says B.S.—you better believe it.

SUCCESS

Confidence is when "if you care enough to send the very best"— you go yourself.

> It's nice to stay a winner,
> A fact we shouldn't fuzz;
> But I'd rather be a has-been—
> Than be a never-was!

Behind every successful man there's a woman saying: "What do you mean you're going to be late for dinner?"

Success is when you get along with your staff and ahead of your competitors.

Success is the stuff that comes neatly wrapped in a package of work.

The problem with being a success is, you have to keep working at it. There is no parking on Easy Street.

If I ever signed a contract for a million dollars a year, I'd be inclined to get a little ostentatious. The first thing I'd do is throw a big party and use five-dollar bills as coasters.

Real success is the black construction firm that builds every part of a house but one. They have a white subcontractor come in to do the windows.

Hectic? I'm busier than a politician's pocket!

SUMMER

You can tell the summer is almost here. Kids are wearing much lighter clothes to watch television.

It was so hot at *Playboy*, the centerfold took off her staple.

I hate hot weather. This is the time of year when I always feel like going to sleep and leaving a call for September.

This is the time of the year when millions of city dwellers go up to the roofs of their apartment buildings, stretch out in their bathing suits, and get a sootburn.

Summer is a very fulfilling season. It's when a man who wants to smell like a man—does.

August is the month, if your kids ask you where you're going, "Crazy!" isn't an adequate answer.

By the end of summer, mothers are so shook up it's amazing. Like last week our oldest daughter wanted to get married and my wife said: "Sure!" What makes it so amazing—the kid's ten! . . . How do you tie old shoes to the back of a skateboard?

If you really want to bug your wife, *now's* the time to put up the storm windows.

This summer I'm sending my kids out to work because I want them to have all the things I didn't have when I was a kid—fives, tens, and twenties.

It always worries me when I see a swimming pool presided over by a sixteen-year-old lifeguard. They always look like they got their Red Cross certificate for Tanning.

SUPERMAN

I don't know if this is an appropriate time to bring it up, but I have good news and bad news about Superman. The good news is, he's always going into phone booths to undress. The bad news is, they're never vacant.

Can you imagine changing your clothes in phone booths in this kind of weather? Superman is the only one I know who gets sympathy notes from brass monkeys.

Would somebody please tell me where Superman gets the clothes he changes into? Not once have I ever seen a phone booth with a hanger.

You know what worries me? What if Clark Kent goes into a phone booth and changes into the wrong clothes? . . . Instead of an "S" on his chest, it says FRUIT OF THE LOOM?

And have you noticed that Superman never goes back for Clark Kent's clothes? He just leaves them in phone booths. In the last year alone, $42,000 worth of pants, vests, and jackets! I happen to know that every night three people include Superman in their prayers—Hart, Schaffner, and Marx!

Superman is the fella who's always running around in the red, orange, and blue outfit. I don't know where he gets his ideas on color coordination, but I think it's from M&Ms.

I don't want to quibble, but I think Superman gets a lot more credit than he deserves. I mean, if you wore the same outfit for forty years, you'd be strong too!

Superman is the only one I know who gets two minutes and fifteen seconds out of a Five-Day Deodorant Pad.

One thing leads to another. It's undressing in phone booths that makes it possible for Superman to leap over tall buildings in a single bound. You ever back into a cold coin box?

Personally, I can't get too worked up over the fact that Superman flies. If you're retired, so does savings.

Superman is more powerful than a locomotive. Of course, with Amtrak, that's not saying too much.

What kind of a world are we living in? I happen to know that Superman carries Mace.

My favorite is Lois Lane, who has seen Clark Kent and Superman for over forty years and still doesn't know they're the same person. Lois Lane is a perfect 36—and that's just her I.Q.

TANNING

Have you ever been to one of those tanning clinics? A tanning clinic is where you just stand there and get burned from all sides. It's a little like Wall Street.

For the first time in history, people are having their baby shoes bronzed and their birthday suits too.

You have to be very careful with tanning. They say that if you stay out in the sun too long it can affect you. Which could explain some of the candidates from California.

I won't say what all this does to your skin but if you're invited to a masquerade party—all you have to do is put a clasp in your belly button and go as an attaché case.

TAX CUTS

This has really been a wonderful year. For the first time in history, more taxes were trimmed than trees.

I'm always intrigued by something that's called an $——— billion tax cut and, when you figure it out, your share is $6.92. . . . I mean, I've had bigger cuts from envelope flaps.

Personally, I'm very grateful for the tax cut Congress voted. Then again, I thank muggers for leaving me carfare.

Tell me—how do we know it's a tax cut? What if it's a going-out-of-business sale?

TAXES

This is the time of year when taxpayers need all the help they can get—like an orthopedic checkbook.

The tax code is unique. It's the only code that breaks people.

Then there's the very wealthy taxpayer who turned down an invitation to attend a state dinner at the White House. Didn't want to eat with the help.

I won't say what it's like being a middle-income taxpayer but Charmin isn't the only thing that's being squeezed.

This is called Isometric Poverty. Every day you're pushed a little further into it!

Every time I look at what I have to pay in taxes, it scares me shirtless!

I have nothing against withholding. It's just that sometimes I wish a little more of my take-home pay would make it.

Remember when "It's just something you have to live with" was a doctor referring to our ailments? Now it's an accountant referring to our taxes.

But when next you're inclined to complain, just remember that some countries are still reluctant to show "The Waltons"—because it would make their people envious.

TEACHING

There are a lot of references to teaching in the Bible. For instance, it says that Jesus raised Lazarus from the dead. I've had students like that myself.

We know a teacher who's kinda discouraged. She claims there are only three valid reasons for being a teacher—July, August, and Christmas.

Teachers are much more candid than they used to be. During Open School Week, I walked up to a teacher who was watching two six-year-olds yelling and screaming and jumping up and down on a seesaw. I said, "Aren't they something?" She said, "Yes. I wish I had a dozen like them." I said, "How many do you have?" She said, "Three dozen."

TEENAGERS

People knock adolescence but there are some definite advantages to being sixteen years old. For one thing, all the tunes they hear on Muzak are new.

> I can't understand why our teenagers
> Use eye shadow—it's all the rage;
> Some achieve premature glamour—
> The rest premature middle age.

Parents of teenagers have now come up with an early warning system for pregnancy. It's called a date.

I always feel sorry for the caterer at a teenage wedding. What wine goes with Twinkies?

The good news is how much in modern life is inspired by the wisdom of the ages. The bad news is, the ages are between twelve and twenty-one.

They say sound travels much slower than light and that's so. Sometimes the things you say when your kids are teenagers only reach them when they're in their forties.

Pimples are a real problem for kids. When I was fifteen, if I spent as much time looking at books as I looked at mirrors, I'd be another Einstein!

Teenagers are people who hear the word "loafers" and think of shoes. Parents are people who hear the word "loafers" and think of teenagers.

The biggest problem in having kids is not another mouth to feed. It's sixteen years later, another mouth to listen to.

TELEPHONES

Once a month it happens.
It almost makes me ill,
Each time I finish paying
Alexander Graham's Bill!

I don't know what this world is coming to. I have a telephone answering service that never has any messages. It doesn't want to get involved.

I'm against phones with six buttons on them. I say that if God had meant us to have six phone lines He would have given us twelve lips.

Electronic wizardry has created junk phone calls and electronic wizardry can deal with junk phone calls. All you have to do is program your answering machine to go (RASPBERRY).

My brother-in-law said he got a junk phone call today. I think somebody offered him a job.

As anyone with teenagers will tell you, junk phone calls go both ways.

TELEVISION

I'm a firm believer in cable TV. To get me to watch some of the shows, you'd have to use chains.

Each year, on a special Sunday in May, we honor the one who raises our children, instills in them the moral concepts and attitudes that will forever guide their lives, and is their constant companion and solace in times of need—our television set.

Television programming always seems to be based on the Acupuncture Theory—each network trying to stick it to the other.

I don't know why but there's something about this new TV season that reminds me of the inscription on the Statue of Liberty. That part about the wretched refuse.

If the average TV season insults your intelligence, this year it's a regular Don Rickles.

I can't get over the sheer immensity of the new TV season—150 new personalities, 38 new series, 2 new plots.

More and more, television is going in for fictionalized accounts based on true incidents. Some are called miniseries. Others are called press conferences.

Television is the device that acquaints you with all the things going on in the world you could be a part of if you weren't sitting there watching television.

Television is doing wonderful things these days. Did you see that documentary about the I.R.S.? It's called *The Invasion of the Booty Snatchers*.

I don't think violence on TV affects the viewer and I'll break anybody's arm who says otherwise.

Don't you kid yourself. There's a lot of violence on TV. Last night in just one program I saw punching and pounding and twisting and slapping. I'll never watch Julia Child make bread dough again.

I think there is too much sex and violence on TV. Every time I want to watch the sex, my wife gets violent.

I'll say one thing for the new season on TV: it's dirt cheap.

One show is so sexy, they say if you watch it too much you'll go blind.

The most economical way to watch some of the new programs on TV is with a very old set. The set is black and white but you turn colors.

I always wanted to be a commentator on one of those televised golf tournaments—but I flunked Whispering.

I know a fella who's eighty-five years old and he's still working. Every time he starts thinking about retiring, he watches daytime TV and changes his mind!

They say that very few people ever learn from experience and that's right. I saw a freight train go off the track on the Six O'Clock News—and darned if it didn't happen again on the Seven O'Clock News.

I'm fascinated by "60 Minutes." It's the only show on television where seconds and people get ticked off.

> If you have a little lisp,
> Your speaking voice it alters;
> Consider all whose words are crisp—
> Passed by for Barbara Walters!

I can't help but wonder if life wouldn't be a lot better if we could live it in one-hour segments—with a little introduction by Alistair Cooke.

If you're my age, watching the Miss America pageant is like going to a travelogue. It's nice to see so many places you ain't never going to get to in person.

I'm against video tape recorders. I just don't believe God intended us to watch the Super Bowl and the third game of the World Series on the same day.

TELEVISION COMMERCIALS

In advertising the truth will out—and sometimes never return.

Have you ever really studied those commercials on TV? Everybody looks like they've just come down with terminal smiling.

And all of this because they guzzle soft drinks. Maybe they just want to show their teeth while they still have some.

Television commercials are a unique experience. For the first time in history, indigestion is a spectator sport.

When I'm watching television and I see what that huge company claims it's doing just for little ole me, I say, "Incredibull!"

I always thought "a nagging pain" was an efficiency expert.

I wish those aspirin commercials wouldn't keep using the phrase "for fast, fast, fast relief." It always sounds as if they've put an express line in at welfare.

I don't want to brag, but I am so adorable, so cuddly, so irresistible —yesterday I was walking down a supermarket aisle and a package of Charmin squeezed *me!*

I'm just amazed at some of the things they're selling on TV—like lemon rinse. It's for people who have this uncontrollable urge to rinse lemons.

There are two types of women in this world: those with iron-poor blood who are drawn to Geritol—and those with iron-rich blood who are drawn to magnets.

I tend to worry about strange things—like, where are the germs that cause good breath?

TENNIS

They say there are now 35 million tennis players in the United States. Wrong! There are 165 tennis players. The rest are waiting for courts.

I've been suffering from a terrible case of tennis elbow. Last Saturday my wife won and she's been nudging me ever since.

A little advice for the beginner: tennis is an incredibly strenuous game that calls for chasing a ball with a racket for hours on end—so it's best to start off with mixed doubles. Get a trayful of drinks and watch.

TEXAS

I was in Texas once and heard a discouraging word. It was from an elocutionist.

Pom poms are what cheerleaders used to shake until Dallas came up with something better.

People around here have such a nice way of setting you straight. During the Happy Hour, someone asked me where I came from. I said, "I come from the greatest state in the Union." He said, "That's funny. You sure don't sound like a Texan!"

They really overdo it in Texas. I mean, who gets buried in a three-room casket?

We drove through Texas on our vacation and we couldn't help but notice all the signs saying: WATCH OUT FOR CROSSING CATTLE! WATCH OUT FOR HIGH WINDS! WATCH OUT FOR FLASH FLOODS! Last Tuesday so many Texans were watching out for crossing cattle, high winds, and flash floods—somebody stole Fort Worth.

We've got to do something because Texas is running out of oil. It really is. I just saw a 10-quart hat.

I happen to know that Texas has so much natural gas, you have to go over to Arizona to light a cigar!

They do a lot of serious drinking down in Texas. In Texas, the beans that keep getting refried are human.

THANKSGIVING

This Thanksgiving try to be grateful for practical things. Like, be thankful the post office doesn't handle prayers.

Can you imagine Thanksgiving dinner today if the Pilgrims had landed in Africa instead of America? You ever try to stuff a hippopotamus?

If you're a turkey, the Bermuda Triangle is Thanksgiving.

A Department of Agriculture report said there may not be enough turkeys to go around. Voters would disagree.

Thanksgiving dinner: the pause that refleshes.

Thanksgiving dinner is a unique experience. It's like an orgy that's rated G.

Mark my words, the first person who comes up with a 22-pound turkey that can be cooked in a toaster—has it made!

The average mother takes two whole days to prepare for Thanksgiving dinner but most kids don't really care. I have taken an informal but exhaustive poll of kids and have come to the conclusion that, if Twinkies came with drumsticks, all turkeys would die of old age.

Our kids love Thanksgiving dinner and it's all because we've learned how to draw a compromise between the old and the new. We have a 22-pound turkey—but we stuff it with Big Macs.

Last year we let the kids make Thanksgiving dinner and it really brought home how unimaginative my wife and I have been all these years. Not once have we ever thought of using Twinkies for stuffing.

This may be hard to believe, but the Rockefellers only began to eat their Thanksgiving dinner on December 2nd. When they sat down, someone suggested that they count their blessings.

Rich? Some people have stuffing. They have a walk-in turkey!

A sadist is anyone who sits down with twenty ravenous people at a table loaded with Thanksgiving turkey, stuffing, roast potatoes, candied yams, and cranberry sauce—and takes fifteen minutes to say grace.

I come from a family of eaters. Real eaters. For instance, last Thanksgiving we had a 26-pound turkey. Oh, I know what you're thinking. Lots of families have 26-pound turkeys. As an appetizer?

Can you imagine paying (CURRENT PRICE) a pound for turkey? For the first time in history mothers are giving their kids candy. "Here, ruin your appetite!"

Some people will do anything to cut down on the expense of a Thanksgiving dinner. Like, before my uncle starts carving the turkey, he always asks, "Seconds, anyone?"

We bought a 23-pound turkey for Thanksgiving but fortunately we didn't have to empty the refrigerator to make room for it. Paying for it did that.

I still haven't made up my mind about last Thanksgiving. We either had pheasant under glass or turkey overpriced.

I always try to invite someone to Thanksgiving dinner who's less fortunate than I am—and each year they get harder to find.

Believe me, it isn't easy inviting the guests, cleaning the house, doing the shopping, baking the pies, calming the kids, serving the drinks, and cooking a seven-course dinner for a houseful of relatives. It's why each Thanksgiving millions of turkeys are stuffed with bread crumbs and millions of housewives are stuffed with Valium.

I'll never forget the very first Thanksgiving dinner my wife ever made. Her cookbook said to wrap the turkey in aluminum foil, put it in a 325-degree oven, and roast until brown. Well, sir, fourteen hours later that aluminum foil was still silver.

My wife is never quite sure when to take a turkey out of the oven. Fortunately, her mother is a very practical instructor. She says the minute that turkey looks like it spent four weeks at Miami Beach—take it out!

You can always tell a considerate hostess at a Thanksgiving dinner. She's the one who has Pepto-Bismol on draft.

Indigestion is always a problem after Thanksgiving dinners. It's the only day of the year when if you hear a thunderous, earsplitting roar it isn't a tornado—it's Uncle Louie.

And after you've finished gorging yourself on a huge Thanksgiving dinner, be sure to watch one of those teeth-rattling, bone-crushing, gut-busting football games on television. It always helps to know that someone is in more pain than you are.

I'm not much of a drinker but after a Thanksgiving dinner I like to go out and get one big belt—because the one I'm wearing no longer fits!

The conceit of human beings is beyond belief. We go into a butcher shop, shell out our last $20 for a bird—and *we're* calling *it* a turkey!

You know all those turkeys saturated with butter? This year, for the first time, they're also going to have turkeys saturated with peanut butter. One bite and you say, "Well, shut mah mouth!" Five, and your problem is opening it.

One Thanksgiving I called up a butcher in San Francisco and I said, "What do you have that's plump, juicy, and tender?" He said, "Thpeaking!"

As the oven said to the Thanksgiving turkey: "I'm hot for your body!"

The last week in November is when the Baskin-Robbins Flavor-of-the-Month is Leftover.

This turkey was so small, we had a unique problem—leftunders.

TOURISTS

Nowadays it's easy to tell tourists in Europe. They're the ones throwing cold water on their credit cards to keep them from overheating.

I wonder how many tourists come over from Scotland, get a yearning for home-country food, look up a restaurant with a good Scottish name—and go to McDonald's?

And as every tourist quickly finds out, the softness and texture of European bathroom tissue is like the very next thing to American bathroom tissue—the wrapper.

One week with this tissue and H needs more preparation.

TOURS

This year the big thing is package tours. If you want to go on a tour, it's going to cost you a package.

A tour bus is when 44 people spend a few thousand dollars each to share the same space—if it was an elevator, you'd wait for the next one.

We had a fairly typical vacation. A 14-day, 5-country tour followed by a 24-payment, 2-year loan.

Who can ever forget those immortal words from the Statue of Liberty? "Give me your tired, your poor, your huddled masses yearning to breathe free!" It used to refer to immigrants. Now it refers to Americans who have just spent fourteen days on a tour bus.

Ask any vacationer who has just returned from a 14-day, 8-country tour and they'll tell you, "Back is beautiful!"

A European tour is a religious experience. You spend half the time going through cathedrals and the other half praying—that they won't make you go through another cathedral.

But Paris is still the City of Romance. It's the only city where the package tours offer you 6 days and 9 nights.

TRAVEL

Travel is relaxing. I can prove it. Yesterday I got so tense I called up an airline to take a vacation trip. I got a recorded announcement that all lines were busy; not to hang up; my call would be handled by the first available clerk; and for the next twenty-five minutes I listened to Broadway show tunes. I got so relaxed, I canceled the trip.

I love those foreign-language books that give you helpful phrases. They always start off with things like: "Help! Get me a doctor! Help! Get me a policeman!" It's great if somebody is trying to steal your appendix!

Another useful phrase is, "Good evening, sir or madam—as the case may be." The way kids are dressing these days, sometimes that's as close as you can get!

The big difference between airlines and buses is the way they handle baggage. Airlines lose your baggage by sending it to exotic cities all over the world. You can never lose your baggage on a bus because it travels with you. It's only when you step out of the bus terminal that you lose it.

I don't want to complain about the amenities on a bus, but I happen to know that medical insurance companies now have a special policy for people who try to use the washroom on a bus going 70 miles an hour. . . . The claim forms are rather interesting. They all start off with: YOU FRACTURED YOUR WHAT?

I've finally figured out why airports make you walk so far to get to the plane. It's their way of giving your luggage a head start.

It's not that I distrust the airlines but I'm now working on a suitcase that will drop little bits of bread behind it as a trail.

I have one suitcase that's been lost so many times, the minute it sees an airport it starts to cry.

I'm one of those unlucky travelers. For instance, I've been to Europe three times. My luggage, once.

I don't want to complain, but I have suitcases that have traveled 9000 more miles than I have.

The thing that has always puzzled me about lost luggage is, what do the airlines do with it? I keep having this crazy feeling that somewhere, deep in the recesses of the Rocky Mountains, there's a cavern with twenty-three years' accumulation of suitcases, trunks, and garment bags—60% of the world's proven reserve of lost luggage!

There are certain basic rules of travel you should be aware of. Like, when they say you should travel light—they mean your suitcase, not your wallet.

We complain about travel now but can you imagine what it was like in biblical times? You ever ride on a charter donkey?

An African safari is like a reverse smorgasbord. You pay $5000 for all that can eat you.

A European visitor was telling me how bad the droughts are over there and how sorry he was to see it was even worse over here. I said, "Why do you think that?" With only the hint of a smile, he pointed at a car driving by pulling a boat.

I love to visit Scandinavia because everything is so spotless. I was in one town that was so clean, it had three washrooms—MEN, WOMEN, and PIGEONS!

Spouses are like traveler's checks. If you're going to Paris, Monte Carlo, or Las Vegas—"you can't leave home without them."

You know what really hurts when you go to Hong Kong? All those junk souvenirs marked MADE IN AMERICA.

Two weeks in Europe is a family experience. You go like the Rockefellers and come back like the Waltons.

We just got back from a trip to Europe. We spent most of our time studying ruins—our budget.

TUITION

First there were killer sharks. Next there were killer ants. Then there were killer bees. And now Hollywood is working on a disaster movie just for parents—*Killer Tuition!*

I got the tuition bills for our three kids in the mail this morning. I'll tell you one thing: it sure beats prune juice!

If your kids go to a school that charges $106 a point, you begin to wonder if your head isn't what the point is on.

They now figure the average college student goes through 265 books in four years—260 are text and the rest are bank.

One of my kids is studying to be a doctor and he says he's going to pay me back every cent with free medical care. I don't ever want to be that unhealthy!

UNEMPLOYMENT

CLIMATOLOGIST: a weatherman who guesses right.
UNEMPLOYED: a weatherman who guesses wrong.

The boss said we might be laying more people off next week. Tell me, what wine goes with panic?

I think the Administration is taking the wrong approach when it comes to unemployment. The President has said there should be a job for everyone who wants to work. That would miss my brother-in-law completely.

When you look for a job, it's always a little awkward getting character references. Don't take my word for it—ask Nixon.

The way the new batch of graduates is being received by business and industry, some of them must be getting the feeling their degrees came from Who U?

July is when a lot of students receive another commencement address—the location of the unemployment office.

UTILITY BILLS

I think I'm finally beginning to understand the metric system. A meter is three feet, three inches long. Unless it's a gas meter, in which case it can be two or three hundred dollars high.

I don't want to complain about the gas and electric company but either their estimates are wrong or their computer is in heat!

I finally figured out the proper greeting for the fella who sits in that remote office estimating your gas and electric bill: "High!"

I don't know where they get the people who estimate these bills but I think it's where income tax auditors go when they turn mean.

My gas bill was so high I wanted to end it all but I was afraid to use the oven.

VACATIONS

A vacation is the shortest distance between two paychecks.

Last year we discovered a vacation spot that's convenient to get to, comfortable, relaxing, where we don't have to get dressed up, and that's priced within our budget. It's called the living room.

Whenever we go away on vacation we always make sure the house looks lived in. We have an automatic timer hooked up to a tape deck. Then we prerecord an argument.

To watch your neighbor's vacation slides, all you need are three things: patience, goodwill, and the ability to yawn through your belly button.

What I like about a vacation is, it fills so much of your year. If you take your vacation in August—you get your slides back in September; your bills back in October; your health back in November; and your luggage back in December.

Who can ever forget Winston Churchill's immortal words: "We shall fight on the beaches, we shall fight on the landing grounds, we shall fight in the fields and in the streets, we shall fight in the hills." Sounds like our last family vacation.

A two-week vacation is when you go away to live and your plants stay home to die.

Vacations are a real problem for plants—particularly if you talk to them. After three days your amaryllis is turning to your begonia and saying: "Where's Big-mouth?"

They say that if you take a European vacation it shows that you have money. Wrong! It shows that you *had* money!

I won't say how expensive things are, but remember when Richard III said, "A horse! A horse! My kingdom for a horse"? Well, they're still charging those prices.

Some things just naturally follow. For instance: "A day without wine is like a day without sunshine." And a day without sunshine is like the start of your vacation.

When I get back from a vacation, I always make it a point to save the last traveler's check for an emergency—like eating.

VALENTINE'S DAY

Do something special on Valentine's Day. It's the first day of the rest of your wife.

I love those Valentine cards that say: TO THE ONE I LOVE MOST. In Hollywood they're sent to mirrors.

Little kids are an important part of the Valentine's Day market. You can tell that by the colognes retailers carry. Products like Evening in Des Moines.

When I was eight years old I bought my mother a bottle of cologne that had so much alcohol in it—you could either wear it, burn it, or drink it.

Our son, the freshman, made a special trip home for Valentine's Day—and gave his mother something that brought tears to her eyes. A heart-shaped five-pound box of laundry.

VITAMINS

A lot of people are confused about the difference between generic and brand names, but it's really rather simple. A generic name would be vitamin E. The brand name would be Honeymoon Helper.

It just shows you what can happen when your vitamin E gets a little ahead of your yogurt.

Incidentally, it's not known as vitamin E anymore—Macho Helper!

I never quite realized how many iron supplements my wife was taking until one morning she got out of bed, stretched and slowly turned north.

WALL STREET

I'll tell you how bad things are on Wall Street. My broker is in a basement office. Yesterday he opened the window and tried to jump up!

Please, Wall Street, stand up straight. I don't think I could take another slump.

Wall Street is the only street I know where you have to go upstairs to get mugged.

I understand Wall Street is putting together its own television show. It's a telethon for Terminal Profits.

Nowadays the only people who are cleaning up on Wall Street are brokers with dogs.

This is a very pregnant time on Wall Street. If you're an investor, the pains are coming every few minutes.

You can tell when Wall Street is having a 100-million-share day. Someone calls up and says, "I want to buy 20,000 shares of General Motors." And the broker says, "Take a number."

WASHINGTON, D.C.

I think it's wrong to say Washington doesn't have a sense of humor. Look at all the politicians they address as "The Honorable."

In Washington they put out special advisories to warn you of potential disasters. They tell you when snow is falling, hurricanes are coming, or Congress is meeting.

How about this weather? The snow was so deep in Washington, three crats couldn't find their bureau.

There's a reason why ballet is so popular in Washington. They're just not used to seeing anyone on their toes.

Washington, D.C., has an interesting effect on people who are suddenly catapulted into power. It's called the Amazon River Syndrome. They start off small and humble but they end up with a big mouth.

They're making a new movie about Washington and something happened on the set that was rather disturbing. They were filming a scene where a politician had to make an ethical decision—so they sent in a stuntman.

If you live in Washington long enough, your credibility has stretch marks.

Then there's the tourist who visited Washington, stopped a resident on the street, and said, "Pardon me, but could you tell me which side the State Department is on?" The Washingtonian just said, "Ours, I think."

Washington is a fascinating place to visit. Washington is the only city I know where they have a statue of a naked goddess called Truth—and if you look real close, you can see the stretch marks.

WEALTH

Rich? Who else do you know has water skis that sleep six?

I'm not much of a debater. I found that out in the middle of a debate with one of the Rockefellers, when I said, "Oh yeah? Well, if you're so smart, why aren't you rich?"

If there's one thing I hate, it's ostentation. I can't stand people who flaunt their money. What's that? What time is it? (LOOK AT YOUR WATCH.) It's three diamonds after twelve.

Rich? Who else do you know has Perrier on the knee?

WEATHER

Sometimes it makes me hot. Sometimes it just sends cold chills up and down my spine. It's so round, so firm, so responsive to the touch, I just can't keep my hands off it. I don't think people should feel that way about a thermostat, do you?

I'll tell you how I look at weather reports. I still think Fahrenheit is doing a pretty good job, but that fella Celsius is murder!

I think they ought to do something about all that violence on TV. For instance, ban the weather report.

This is Express Checkout Line weather—8 degrees or less.

I'll say one thing for our paper boy. No matter how bad the storms were, his record was as good as when the sun was shining. Missed six days out of seven.

We have a very cautious Weather Bureau. For instance, on Monday they predicted a 70% chance of Tuesday.

Abraham Lincoln said, "You can't fool all of the people all of the time." Abraham Lincoln never worked for the Weather Bureau.

Meteorologists said it was one of the worst storms in history. Dorothy and Toto said, "Eh!"

Thanks to this weather, we finally know how to spell "relief"— J-U-L-Y.

America is still the land of opportunity. Where else could you go from owning a ranch home in Minnesota to a houseboat in Mississippi—and never have to move?

To make sure this never happens again, the government is proposing a five-year flood control program. It's a combination of small dams and big blotters.

I wish they wouldn't show these films of the flooding on the Seven O'Clock News. It always reminds my wife of the last time I tried to fix the sink.

A hurricane is when the garage door stays in place but the house goes up.

The drought has been so bad that some communities have a brand-new way of celebrating Halloween. They're going to fill a vat with apples and bob for water.

Water shortages create all kinds of different, urgent and monumental problems. Like, what do old ladies throw on two dogs?

WEATHER (COLD)

I can't understand all this talk about cold weather. I don't think the weather is that cold and neither does my wife Nanook.

A radio station on the beach at Waikiki has a feature called the Happiness Minute. It's the weather report from Duluth, Minnesota.

I feel sorry for the folks in Minnesota. I mean, they really know what cold is. You ever see a blowtorch freeze?

In Minnesota, a cold snap is what happens to your pipes.

Minneapolis is so cold, people just sneer at the weather. They look at a thermometer and say: "How low can you get!"

I won't say what the weather in Chicago has been like, but flags up there now have forty-nine stars and a muffler.

There are three reasons why so many people spend the winter in Chicago. It's stimulating, it's colorful, and you can't start the car to get out.

On these 20-below mornings, you really have to feel sorry for a priest trying to start his car. He just doesn't have the vocabulary for it.

There's nothing wrong with this weather that a jumper cable from Florida to Massachusetts couldn't cure.

Something's got to be done about this cold weather. Something dramatic—like weather-stripping the Canadian border.

It's so cold, it used to be your enemies told you to go to hell. Now it's your friends.

The head cold season is here—when everywhere you go you see people with Adidas noses.

Last night it was so cold, I put on my coat to take out the garbage —and it didn't want to go!

Last night it was so cold, I made my wife quit Weight Watchers.

This is the kind of weather where it helps to have the right size comforter on your bed—80 by 108—or 38 by 22 by 36.

Last night it was so cold, my wife's headache cleared up.

We had a formal dinner and you know how you're supposed to serve red wine at room temperature? We did. We served it on a stick.

(COLDEST CITY) is now the world's only Popsicle with a mayor.

(COLDEST CITY) is a wonderful experience for anyone who has ever wanted to live inside a Good Humor truck.

It's ridiculous. You sit in a room this cold for two hours and you're ready to be Baskin-Robbins' newest flavor!

When it comes to keeping warm in this kind of weather, nothing beats a thermal blonde.

They just gave an award for the toughest, bravest, most fearless person in the United States today. It went to an exhibitionist in (COLDEST CITY).

WEIGHT WATCHERS

Weight Watchers are firm believers in the Hippocratic Oath. Every week they take an Oath not to look like a Hippo.

When it comes to melting pots, you just can't beat Weight Watchers.

You can always spot a temptress at Weight Watchers. She's the one who puts a dab of gravy behind her ears.

Thanks to Weight Watchers, you don't have to go to Las Vegas to lose at tables.

The people in Weight Watchers are very polite. They're ready to give their seat to anyone.

WHITE HOUSE

At the White House they have this big map of the world with a pin at every trouble spot. Yesterday they sent out for more pins.

I won't say how this Administration is meeting the issues, but they're now calling the White House "Dodge City"!

They say no two snowflakes are alike. The White House has that same problem with policy statements.

Californians love hot tubs. That's when a group of people get into hot water up to their ears. We have the same thing in Washington. It's called the White House.

I won't say what's happening at the White House but they're now calling it the Oval Bunker.

Is it true that last week a businessman in Chicago made a phone call and got the White House by mistake? He said, "Is this the Success Institute?" And the operator said, "Boy, have you got the wrong number!"

This could go down in history as the Red Flannel Underwear Administration—one flap after another.

The scene is a cocktail party in Washington. Two fellas are introduced to each other and after a certain amount of small talk one says, "Have you heard the latest White House joke?" The second fella holds up his hand and says, "No—and before you begin, I think you should know that I work at the White House." The first fella says, "Not to worry. I'll tell it very slowly."

It doesn't make sense. Like singing "where never is heard a discouraging word" at the White House.

WINES

I don't want to complain but I have found out why they're called wine and cheese parties. You taste the wine and you say, "Cheese!"

This weather is a problem to gourmets. They say you should serve wine at room temperature, but who likes boiled Bordeaux?

Chicago has an apartment building that's over a hundred stories high. This building is so tall, the wine cellar is on the thirty-eighth floor.

If you really want to upset the owner of a fine French restaurant, order a bottle of Château Lafite Rothschild 1969—and two straws.

Californians drink a lot of wine. A *lot* of wine! You think that's smog over Los Angeles? Wrong! Fruit flies!

Chianti is more than a wine. It's Italian Valium!

I bought a one-gallon jug of wine for $1.98 and it came from a very unusual vintage—Tuesday.

WINTER

It's been a long, hard, confining winter, and so yesterday my wife and I just felt we had to do something to raise our morale. Something that would at least give us a ray of hope for better days ahead. So we packed our kid's suitcase for summer camp.

Winter is when the mean temperature is.

I know this has been a very cold winter but I never really worried about it until this fella down the street named Noah started building a furnace 300 cubits long, 50 cubits wide, and 30 cubits high.

It's been a bad winter but I don't really think I have cabin fever. It's like I was telling my TV set this morning. I said, "George—"

I never have a problem during the winter and it's all because of the Head Cold Martini—three parts gin and one part chicken soup.

Don't think of it as winter. Think of it as a 90-day cooling-off period.

My wife has spent the entire winter in an outfit that looks like it came from Frederick's of Siberia.

Don't misunderstand. She has not lost her femininity. You can tell that by the black lace on her surplus air force parka!

November is when every mail brings you two more Christmas catalogs for cheese. I get so confused, I don't know whether we're celebrating the birth of Christ or cholesterol.

January is the underwear time of the year. When the Christmas bills start arriving, everyone has the shorts.

A UFO has never landed in (SNOWBOUND CITY) in January—proving once and for all that there is intelligent life on other planets.

WOMEN

God created woman from man's rib. Now here's the plan, fellas: we start charging rent for that rib—retroactively!

There's a brand-new perfume for girls who go crazy over Italian food. It's called Eau de Provolone.

Well, as Lady Godiva's horse said: "That's a new one on me!"

I don't want to start any trouble, but if women are so smart, how come they always dance backward?

The saddest story ever told is about the girl who brought her 1984 diary back to the bookstore. The clerk asked her, "What's wrong?" She said, "Nothing happened."

You know the girl you're dating is too young when she orders a grasshopper with that little straw—and then blows bubbles in it.

I don't ask for much out of life. I just want to meet a girl with a million-dollar figure and be nickeled and dimed to death.

I used to have a girlfriend who was an Egyptologist. Every time I made a wrong move, she said, "Tut! Tut!"

If your wife does nothing but talk about the Douglas fir, it means one of two things: either she's become a nature lover or Sarah Douglas got a new mink.

Women are so unreasonable. My wife gets mad because every Saturday night I take a bath with bubbles in it. I mean, if Bubbles doesn't mind, why should she?

If your wife isn't feeling well, there is one quick way to cure her: offer to help with the housework. My wife had an almost miraculous recovery when I started to vacuum the windows.

My wife is always looking for bargains. For instance, we have a set of dishes that say DRY-CLEAN ONLY.

Historians have just discovered that Brigham Young was not a polygamist. He only had one wife—but she had forty-two wigs.

WOMEN'S LIB

Women's Lib has come up with a very interesting argument. They say, if God was satisfied with Adam, how come He made Eve so different?

A number of women in our neighborhood are getting together tonight for a consciousness-raising session. That's what they call it. Their husbands call it a group headache.

The Thanksgiving turkey dinner started off as a symbolic occasion and it still is. I went over to Women's Lib and you should have seen the way they carved up that tom.

I can't understand it. Women's Liberation sent me an invitation to be their keynote speaker. I accepted and I never heard from them again. What makes it so irritating, I even offered to bring along the little woman.

WORKING

I don't mind the additives in food. What gets me are the subtractives in paychecks.

I keep hearing about a mandatory retirement age. I'm still trying to convince my kids there's a mandatory work age.

It's amazing how many people are becoming dedicated to the workaday life. They work a day and say, "This is a life?"

I don't mind trying to keep up with the Joneses, but every now and then, couldn't they make a pit stop?

There's a reason why so many millions and millions of women are entering the labor force. It's called daytime TV.

They say it's mighty hard to find anyone who'll do an honest day's work. You know something? With two-hour lunches, twenty-minute coffee breaks, wash-up time, and washroom time—it's even mighty hard to find an honest day.

I won't say we're overworked, but our lunchroom has a carry-out service and so does our production line.

In my business you get used to putting in long hours. Sometimes I leave the house at half past Captain Kangaroo and get back at quarter to Sermonette.

Whenever the boss sees me putting in overtime he figures it's because of dedication—and he's right. There's my wife, Sarah Dedication; my kids, Laura and Billy Dedication; my dog, Rover Dedication; my house, the Casa Dedication; and the holder of the mortgage, the First National Bank of Dedication.

We had an interesting personnel problem last year. I called in our newest salesman and said, "When we hired you, you told us you never got tired—but every time I go into your office you're sleeping." He said, "Of course. That's why I never get tired!"

X-RATED MOVIES

Hollywood may call them X-rated, but I call them Crossword Puzzle Movies. In the first scene, they're vertical—and for the rest of the picture they come across.

Thanks to X-rated movies, *déjà vu* is now honeymoons.

You're over the hill when you go to an X-rated movie and the first thing you notice is how many girls have had their appendix out.

Hollywood has made its first X-rated mystery and, to maintain the suspense, nobody will be seated during the last ten oo-oo, ee-ee, oh-oh, aahhhhhs.

I was a very naive kid. I'll never forget the first time I saw an X-rated movie. I was very disappointed. I said, "I've heard of jumper cables, but this is ridiculous!"

ZIP CODES

I have nothing against the Zip Code. I just keep hoping that someday the post office will break it.

The postal service wants to add four more digits to the Zip Code. You don't know what that does to a fella who's still calling one of his kids What's-his-name.

Can you imagine a Zip Code that reads 764533248? It'll look like the (WINNING BASEBALL TEAM)'s half of the scoreboard.

Remember the Alamo! Remember the *Maine!* Remember Pearl Harbor! But do we really have to remember a nine-digit Zip Code?

Incidentally, there is no truth to the rumor that the post office got the idea for nine digits from their deficit.